Managing for Ethical–Organizational Integrity

Managing for Ethical–Organizational Integrity

Principles and Processes for Promoting Good, Right, and Virtuous Conduct

Abe J. Zakhem and Daniel E. Palmer

First published in 2012 by
Business Expert Press, LLC
222 East 46th Street, New York, NY 10017
www.businessexpertpress.com

ISBN-13: 978-1-60649-157-7 (paperback)

ISBN-13: 978-1-60649-158-4 (e-book)

DOI 10.4128/9781606491584

A publication in the Business Expert Press Strategic Management collection

Collection ISSN: 2150-9611 (print)
Collection ISSN: 2150-9646 (electronic)

Cover design by Jonathan Pennell
Interior design by Exeter Premedia Services Private Ltd.,
Chennai, India

First edition: 2012

10 9 8 7 6 5 4 3 2 1

Printed in the United States of America.

Abstract

For some time people thought that business and ethics constituted separate and mutually exclusive realms. Businesses that perpetuate such a belief or still hold that "business ethics" is an oxymoron are at risk. Indeed, managers are now being called on to actively promote ethical-organizational integrity. This means understanding the principles that define and creating an organizational culture that measurably encourages ethical conduct. The reason for this shift in paradigm is clear. Ethical-organizational integrity drives long-term company success and sustainable value production, serves to prevent illegal conduct, and best contributes to overall social welfare. This book provides a brief introduction to and general framework for managing for ethical-organizational integrity that will be useful to managers and business students alike.

Keywords

Business ethics, corporate social responsibility, ethics programs, integrity management, legal compliance, stakeholder management

Contents

Introduction

Being a person brings with it serious existential concerns about how we ought to live our lives. To ignore these concerns is to live superficially and without deep meaning, conviction, or integrity. The study of ethics tries to provide critical insight and guidance regarding how we ought to live our lives. More specifically, the study of ethics involves determining what truly constitutes good, right, and virtuous behavior. Correlatively, actually becoming an ethical person means trying to live by the standards and ideals at which we rationally arrive and persuading others to do the same. In this process several questions inevitably arise. To what extent are we obligated to do good for ourselves, others, and society? When seeking that which is good to what extent do we need to respect the rights of other persons? What exactly is a virtue and how do we actually promote virtuous behavior? What ought we to do when conceptions of the good, right, and virtuous conflict? Grappling with these questions and acting on the often challenging implications that answers bring constitutes what Plato famously called an examined life and puts one on the path of a life truly worth living.

As the unexamined life is not worth living in general, so too it is not worth living if we ignore ethics in our professional, business lives. Much of our lives are spent at or thinking about our jobs and the decisions we make in business affect a great number of people not directly involved in our more discrete transactions. After all, business is a complex, interrelated, and exceedingly influential social practice where the impact of a single decision may have profound consequences. Engaging in business without critical regard for the harm we may cause others or the good we can produce, the rights we may infringe upon and the obligations we ought to respect, and how our conduct affects the kind of persons we and others ought to be is unbefitting a life worth living.

Fortunately, there are few who disagree with the belief that we ought to be ethical businesspersons. In philosophical, economic, and even managerial theory the general value and importance of business ethics has never really been denied. Indeed, the moral philosopher and then economist Adam Smith predicated capitalism and the rational pursuit of one's self-interest on the idea that this sort of hedonism best promotes individual and social utility. Smith also appealed to the importance of justice as a virtue and heralded what he and others deemed the natural rights of liberty and property. We ought to leverage our property to help secure our own rational and freely chosen preferences and encourage others to engage in market relations to do the same for themselves. In this sense capitalism and economics have never been value neutral or amoral. Even laissez faire free market capitalists, as it will be demonstrated in chapters 1 and 2, believe that business is a practice designed to ultimately promote the greater good and demands managerial allegiance to at least a limited conception of corporate social responsibility. Economics, business, and management theory is built upon a rather sophisticated ethical framework, relying on normative ideals—one ought do that which is good, respect that which is right, and act virtuously—to justify and promote a complex variety of market transactions.

Despite a great deal of academic accord, thoughts that "business" and "ethics" constitute mutually exclusive domains, or more forcefully that "business ethics" is an oxymoron, have prevailed. Statements like "Business and ethics? There is a contradiction in terms!" may still ring true in many circles. It is important to note, however, that these perceptions and statements speak to judgments regarding the way things are perceived to be and not necessarily to judgments regarding the way things *ought to be*. Philosophers accordingly draw a distinction between empirical or descriptive judgments (how things are) and normative judgments (how things ought to be). This technical, linguistic distinction echoes a degree of common sense likely instilled in us since children. Just because everyone is doing something, like drugs, stealing, or jumping off a bridge, does not mean that everyone ought to. So, the empirical statement that "business ethics is an oxymoron" does not mean that we are saying that "we ought to behave unethically in business," for example, by defrauding shareholders, exploiting child labor, deceiving consumers about product safety issues, engaging in foreign corrupt practices, etc.

The collapses of business giants like Enron, WorldCom, and Tyco and the more recent international financial meltdowns have forcefully shifted public attention to normative considerations in business. Like never before businesses are now called on to change the way things are to better align with the way things ought to be. For managers this means working to establish and maintain ethical corporate cultures, inhibiting unethical conduct, and positively promoting *ethical–organizational integrity*. Despite a considerable degree of imprecision, "managing for ethical-organizational integrity" seems to reflect at least three interrelated assumptions. First, it assumes that having integrity in some way contributes to the wholeness or completeness of a person and leads to consistency in thought and action over time. The second assumption is that this wholeness or completeness derives from having a defined and wholehearted interest in abiding by the right sorts of ethical principles and values. When conducting business, persons with integrity do not, so to speak, check their ethics at the door, lose their integrity when times are tough, and do not merely act in accordance with ethical standards when forced or incentivized. Third, ethical–organizational integrity is achieved by aligning and unifying individual, company, and social ethical standards and expectations. It is critical to highlight at the outset that managing for ethical integrity is necessarily *transformative*.

Transforming a business culture is a difficult task, however, especially when unethical conduct represents the status quo. Given this reality, why should managers go through the trouble of organizational change? Despite more philosophical concerns about a life worth living, shouldn't they simply weather the storm and wait for the business ethics "fad" to run its course? There are two very compelling and pragmatic reasons for not considering the current concern over business ethics a "fad." First, several governmental and other voluntary compliance based standardization initiatives are requiring or otherwise encouraging managing for ethical–organizational integrity. In the United States, for example, the Federal Sentencing Guidelines suggest a particular program for designing and implementing ethics programs with the explicit intent of promoting an ethical–organizational culture.[1] The programmatic suggestions are not mandatory. Nevertheless, companies who adhere to these suggestions receive lesser punishments when illegal and unethical acts occur. Companies who fail to adhere to these suggestions often face rather "draconian" fines.[2] In Japan the Ethics Compliance Management System Standard (ECS 2000) has been designed with similar aims as the American system.[3] Additionally, the international members from the Organization for

Economic Cooperation and Development (OECD) place fostering an ethical culture at the core of its Guidelines for Multinational Enterprises.[4] In short, there is an increasing linkage between ethical–organizational integrity and legal compliance that is becoming codified in national and international standards.

Second, the once arcane notion that "business ethics is good business" is beginning to receive more mainstream attention, especially in managerial theory and organizational practice.[5] Indeed, ethical–organizational integrity is now being seen as crucial for developing and sustaining such things as shareholder trust and lower capital costs, customer satisfaction and loyalty, efficient and productive workforces, employee retention, supply chain value, and environmental and social capital. While short-term corporate performance may sometimes still be enhanced through unethical means, the long-term financial performance and sustainable value production of individual companies, or even whole industries, can be critically tied to their underlying level of ethical–organizational integrity.[6] Companies like Adidas, Ford Motor Company, Standard Chartered Bank, the National Australian Bank, Novo Nordisk, Henkel, and Electrolux contribute to an increasing body of empirical data showing that ethical companies can consistently outperform industry standards.[7] Managing for ethical–organizational integrity and the correlation of embracing sustainable value production is now becoming a competitive necessity. For Unilever Group Chief Executive Officer Patrick J. Cescau the notion of "doing well by doing good" is clear. "Companies that successfully embrace this agenda and integrate it into their businesses and brands will thrive. Those that fail to do so, or react too late to the dramatic social, economic, and environmental changes that are taking place in the world, risk becoming corporate casualties."[8]

Answering the following questions will give a general indication if companies are adequately addressing ethical concerns, are performing as well at they could, or are at risk.

- Does the company have an ethics code of conduct?
- Do mission statements include commitments to legal and ethical conduct?
- Does this commitment reflect stakeholder values and rights?

- Does the company have clear and measurable ethical objectives?
- Are these objectives tied to performance metrics?
- Are ethical requirements present in company policies and procedures?
- Are employees aware of ethics and compliance based requirements?
- Does organizational leadership support ethics initiatives?
- Does the company have a culture that positively supports ethical behavior?
- Is ethical behavior part of the hiring, firing, promotion, and demotion process?
- Are there controls in place to monitor and detect unethical behavior?
- Are there incentives to promote ethical behavior?
- Does the company have a formal ethics and compliance program?

Despite the growing legal and industry acceptance of the importance of managing for ethical–organizational integrity and the increased attention companies are paying to addressing these sorts of questions, there remain two primary challenges. The first challenge is largely philosophical and has to do with determining the exact ethical principles and values to which an organization and its constituents ought to aspire and the corresponding obligations they create. Part of the problem, of course, is that competing notions of ethics and organizational values can be found at play among different discussants of business ethics. In our globalized and pluralistic world, we often find that people simply hold different and often competing ethical beliefs about that which is good, right, and virtuous. Indeed, academics, shareholders, employees, consumers, activists, governments, and their citizens hold different opinions about the ethical rules and obligations that ought to be imposed on businesses. These rules and obligations often differ across companies, nations, cultures, and economies and there appears to be no lasting consensus upon what the proper account of ethical values and standards is. As such, disagreement about organizational ethical identity abound.

Even philosophical conversations and debates about the good, right, and virtuous have likewise failed to produce any overarching agreement as to the complete nature of morality.

Even where there is some general normative consensus, as for instance when most would agree to the propositions that "businesspersons ought to be socially responsible" and "businesspersons ought not to violate basic human rights," there is still much disagreement as to the more positive and concrete duties and practical implications that stem from recognizing these sorts of basic judgments. For example, the meaning of corporate social responsibility, say regarding climate change or sustainability, differs in European and American contexts. We also find disputes about the exact corporate duties that correspond with human rights, say, on such issues regarding whether or not corporations are morally obligated to provide a "living" wage to their employees. There are also disputes as to the kind of character traits we desire in businesspersons. Should businesspersons be cold and callous or more compassionate? As long as these sorts of questions remain unanswered, business and organizational ethics will appear ill-defined and perhaps even inconsistent. This lack of clarity and consistency can even threaten to undercut the very organizational–ethical integrity and unity managers are expected to foster. The problem is exacerbated as multinational companies cross various cultural and economic boundaries.

In order to deal with the problem of defining what business ethics means and actually requires we need to develop certain enduring and action guiding principles. When invited to engage in a more philosophical debate about what principles should be used to determine what is good, right, and virtuous many businesspersons and students gravitate to one of three views. The first is associated with ethical relativism. The relativist tends to hold the following beliefs. I) Persons across different cultures and societies hold different ethical beliefs. II) There is no objective truth in morality. III) We ought to respect personal and cultural beliefs about ethics.[9] In a business context, this means that companies ought to abide by whatever rules are deemed ethical given prevailing, associative or cultural beliefs.

Is this sound reasoning? The first statement seems true. Empirical studies in business, sociology, and anthropology suggest as much. Difficulties associated with holding statements II) and III) come to the surface, however, when considering certain types of problematic cases. Suppose that in some areas of the world cultural or societal beliefs condoned using children of particular ethnicities or classes as slaves. While in general cultural toleration may be virtuous, enslaving children on the basis of race or class and subjecting them to exploitative working conditions seems to be the sort of thing we *ought not* to respect. In saying as much we are making a strong normative claim and suggesting that we should try and compel those who engage in such practices to change their ways. Thus relative to III) practicing toleration does not entail that we are morally obligated to tolerate great forms of injustice.

Regarding II), there do seem to be objective reasons that one can give and defend with regards to normative claims. Why is it wrong to enslave a child based on ethnicity or class? Well, enslaving another person and discriminating on the basis of ethnicity or class violates what many regard as basic human rights concerning equality and equal opportunity. Are there not some rights to which all human beings deserve simply by virtue of being human? Additionally, children are often deemed "morally innocent" and thus it seems wrong to inflict deliberate and arbitrary harm on them. These sorts of reasons provide a much needed basis for moral evaluation and progress. Much of the work in philosophical ethics seeks to rationally justify, clarify, and defend these sorts of objective ethical claims. Furthermore, the statements made in II) and III) are logically inconsistent. Belief III) states that we *ought to respect* personal and cultural ethical beliefs (an objective, normative, and moral claim) and II) states that there are no objective truths in morality (there are no truly objective, normative, and moral claims); both cannot be true. As such, the relativist's position seems to be self-defeating.

While the relativist's position seems faulty on philosophical grounds we also have very good reasons to reject it on practical grounds. Simply put, markets require objective normative commitments to work well or even to work at all. A free market is predicated on clear normative commitments that include truthful financial reporting, recognizing and protecting private property, promoting fair competition and antitrust laws, and honoring contracts. Where free markets exist these specific moral commitments tend to be legally codified and enforced.

The second view commonly used to ground business ethics is expressed in the belief that "if it's legal it's ethical." The obligation that stems from this stance is legal compliance. As in the case of the ethical relativist the legal compliance based position is likewise problematic. Quite obviously there are many examples throughout history where laws were rightfully considered unjust, for example, the case of slavery. Those fighting to abolish slavery and in fact change existing laws were certainly not regarded as acting unethically. The compliance based position should at least be amended to indicate that we are ethically required to follow *just* law.

This, however, is a necessary, but insufficient condition for ethical behavior. The simple fact is that the legal code does not and never will cover all of our ethical commitments. As ethical decision-making often requires contextualization and judgment, ethical obligations simply cannot be fully codified. Additionally, situations on the ground change and the law often lags behind. Consider the case of pharmaceutical clinical trials. The United States, European Union, and most developed countries legally require a patient's informed consent and a commitment to put the subject's welfare above the promise of scientific gain. Suppose that there are underdeveloped countries in which there are no such regulations. In countries without these regulations would it then be ethical to, say, test an unlicensed pharmaceutical on unknowing children in order to determine how harmful the drug's side effects are? Despite being legal there again are very good reasons to conclude that engaging in such clinical trials is unethical and in fact morally repugnant. One certainly does not need to be a philosopher or an ethicist to reach this conclusion. In fact, even among legal compliance specialists the idea that "if it's legal it's ethical" no longer rings true.[10]

The third and once widely held view is that a manager's ethical responsibility is to simply make as much money as they can for their company. As stated by the neoclassical and Nobel Prize winning economist Milton Friedman, a manager's only social responsibility is to maximize profit for shareholders.[11] Unlike the relativist- and compliance-based positions this view is not obviously wrong. In fact, those who support it rightly draw attention to the fact that successful companies in a free market greatly contribute to social welfare, for example, by creating jobs, attracting capital, producing a variety of desirable products, and providing a solid governmental tax base. Despite this realization, the profit maximization and shareholder-centric managerial model falls short on other grounds and structuring an ethical–organizational integrity program around its main principles is ill-advised. Substantiating this conclusion will take some work and we will further examine Friedman's claims in each respective chapter.

In short, this book is designed to help business and business ethics students and managers understand and resolve the problems associated with figuring out what ethics actually requires and to provide sound principles and processes for those interested in managing for ethical–organization integrity. We will use the profit maximization and shareholder centric model as a framework and jumping off point for doing so.

Chapter 1 begins by exploring the thesis that managers require the right sort of conceptual framework when managing for ethical–organizational integrity. We know that in order to be ethical one must do what is good. In business this means being responsible to one's company and also being socially responsible. We begin the chapter by more fully describing the neoclassical framework for business ethics and corporate socially responsibility. While we certainly think that by contributing to a strong economic base company success best promotes overall social welfare, we sharply disagree with the idea that focusing on shareholders and profitability best accomplishes this end. In fact, adhering to the rather myopic neoclassical managerial framework creates more harm than good.

We then explain, develop, and ultimately advocate a stakeholder oriented approach to ethical–organizational management and corporate social responsibility. In short, we find that the stakeholder approach provides a superior framework for understanding and fulfilling the ethical obligations of business and systematically promoting ethical–organizational integrity and company success. The overarching principle behind our approach is that driving long-term company success and sustainable value production (however defined), understanding and trying to meet stakeholder expectations, and developing stakeholder capabilities are mutually dependent. Furthermore, that there are various metrics, including the long-term market value of a firm, stakeholder satisfaction measures, and newly emerging social and environmental capital metrics, that can and do objectively capture managerial performance and prevent managerial opportunism. We then provide a step-by-step procedure for doing what is good in business and suggestions for how to deal with conflict when perceived goods conflict.

Chapter 2 provides philosophical insight into the nature and extent of stakeholder rights and corresponding managerial duties and offers ways to help resolve moral conflict when rights and duties conflict. While chapter 1 focuses managerial efforts on company success, chapter 2 recognizes that there are moral limits to pursuing company success. To help better define these limits and the specific obligations stakeholder rights impose, we introduce some more exacting terminology. As most people recognize some moral rights have a greater significance than others. We recognize as "fundamental rights" those rights that are the weightiest in nature. We take it that these rights are inherently valuable, promote something very important (individual integrity and the integrity of social practices), are under threat, and the duties that they give rise to ought to always be respected.[12] Human rights, for example, fall under the category of fundamental rights. We then recognize "derivative rights" as those rights that may protect something of great importance but nevertheless can be justifiably infringed upon.[13] Privacy rights are of this sort and ought only be infringed upon when doing so protects some other greater good. Additionally, the term "special obligation" is used to characterize relationships with acutely vulnerable and dependent stakeholders and thus demands extra managerial attention and care. We have, for example, special obligations when marketing potentially unsafe products to children. We also distinguish between "positive rights" and "negative rights" to further clarify the nature and extent of managerial responsibilities. This terminology is then used to identify and prioritize the rights of and corresponding obligations due to various stakeholders.

The first two chapters are more philosophically oriented and try to better define and understand what is good and right to do in business. Although technical at times, developing a more philosophically rigorous outlook and vocabulary is a critical task. Philosophy and normative ethics set the foundations upon which business and other social practices are built and it is of utmost importance to start from a solid foundation. If we do not get the foundation right we cannot expect to get the practice of ethics right. Of course, theoretical and philosophical knowledge does not always lead to ethical action. Employees may know very well what ethics requires but lack the character or organizational support to act on their beliefs. Chapter 3 addresses these concerns by first providing some philosophical insight into what constitutes ethical character and how character ought to be developed. In the neoclassical model ethical character extends from the agential relationship said to exist between managers and shareholders. As good agents, managers ought to faithfully, loyally, and with great care attend to shareholder expectations. We again find the neoclassic account to be too myopic. This chapter draws on the philosophy of Aristotle to define and explain the character traits befitting a manager's relationship with various stakeholders, shareholders included.

The second part of chapter 3 identifies the core features of ethics programs that promote intellectual and moral development. These core features are reflected in the various ethics- and compliance-based integrity programs mentioned above, for example, the U.S. Federal Sentencing Guidelines, ECS 2000, and OECD suggestions. This final section is the most practical in nature and will stipulate the processes and provide concrete recommendations for creating and sustaining an ethical-organizational culture.

Along the way we try to substantiate and illustrate the specific claims we make and the views we endorse. We do not, however, claim to resolve all theoretical and practical issues. Both philosophical and practical issues and disputes will inevitably remain unanswered. While there will be certain things a businessperson ought to never do and some things a businessperson ought to always do, there is no single formula or managerial approach that resolves all issues in business and organizational ethics. In our account, being ethical and having integrity is not merely about following discrete rules. Being ethical sets in motion attempts to actively and continually transform practices, persons, and ways of doing business to better reflect philosophically grounded normative ideals. Like other forms of management, managing for ethical–organizational integrity is an art that admits many renderings and narratives and is open to revision and trial and error. With this in mind, we end each chapter with sets of thought-provoking questions that draw attention to current theoretical and practical issues and debates. Does stakeholder theory require a single value function? How much should we value profit? Are corporations persons? Is there a priority of the right over the good? Are shareholder rights primary? Which leadership models better promote organizational integrity? These are some of the theoretical and practical questions that are raised throughout this work.

The emphasis on both normative theory and practice will be of value to business managers, executives, and students and instructors alike. Business professionals may be more interested in the practical implications of this book, but will benefit by understanding the philosophical ground upon which these practices are based. The book could certainly be used in an undergraduate or graduate management class, providing the instructor and students with a general framework to further examine particular business scenarios and cases and develop more concrete business strategies. Likewise, the text provides enough background of the philosophical issues to be used in a more traditionally oriented business ethics course, in which case the instructor could easily use the framework provided in the book to illustrate the practical import of business ethics, while using the normative issues raised as the basis for further in-class and more philosophically oriented discussion and debate. For both management and business ethics students, this book provides a framework that can also be used to analyze a variety of case studies and complements many of the accepted business and business ethics textbooks already in the market.

Finally, it should be noted that this text is written in a style that is meant to engage managers and students in an accessible and pragmatic manner. One of our primary aims in writing this text is to provide an overview of business ethics for managers and students of business that can readily be used to analyze and respond to ethical issues in management. As such, we have tried to limit discussions of purely theoretical issues to those absolutely necessary for a working understanding of the salient aspects of organizational ethics and we have tried to keep scholarly references to a minimum. For readers who are interested in following up on the vast array of academic research pertinent to the issues we discuss, we provide references for further reading at the end of each chapter that provide a good starting point for further research for such interested parties. Likewise, since our aim is to provide a working model for managers to use in developing ethical–organizational integrity, we most definitely promote a particular view of business ethics in this work. As noted above, we do defend this view and contrast it with alternative views where possible, given the aims and intended audience of the book. However, to cover every dispute between the view we advocate and other competing views or to detail all of the theoretical positions that have been taken on these issues would have resulted in us writing a much different, and more narrowly academically oriented, kind of book. Again, where feasible we note where our view significantly differs from others and point readers more interested in such theoretical debates to some of the relevant literature.

We believe that the approach we advocate here is both theoretically justifiable and pragmatically effective, but above all, we hope to have written a work that will provide managers and future managers with a basic understanding of the ethical issues inherent in business and one that gives them the tools to constructively manage for ethical–organizational integrity.

CHAPTER 1

Doing What Is Good

In the introduction we mentioned that promoting ethical–organizational integrity requires doing what is good. Indeed, doing what is good typically involves not only caring for one's self but includes promoting the welfare of others or otherwise promoting that which is deemed valuable (e.g., wealth, health, learning and education, security, sustenance, self-respect, etc.). Thus in business, doing what is good requires more than just advancing private managerial interests or one's career and, in one way or another, involves doing what is good for one's company, and at the same time promoting overall social welfare. But, given the fact that managers have limited resources and that there are times when individual and company interests and social responsibilities conflict, this is no easy task. We thus require a framework and some basic principles for understanding and helping to guide managerial decision-making.

Economists, management theorists, and even philosophers have long tried to provide such a framework. Some claim that corporations ought to serve a very narrow set of interests and in doing so best promote company and social welfare. Others argue that corporations ought to be responsible for trying to meet a wider set of ethical objectives and advance various social causes. The neoclassical managerial framework and articulation of the corporate objective function represents a narrower framework and one that has greatly influenced management theory and practice. The neoclassical model states that managers do best for themselves, their company, and best promote overall welfare, by trying to maximize profits for shareholders. We begin this chapter by presenting some of the central arguments that support this conclusion. We then explain why despite the critical emphasis on doing what is good by promoting company success some of the traditional neoclassical arguments are unsound. The second part of this chapter develops a wider, stakeholder oriented framework for doing what is good in business, upon which we believe that attempts to promote ethical–organizational integrity should be founded.

The Neoclassical Account of Doing Good

The neoclassical management framework came to the forefront of more recent debates about business ethics in response to demands for increased corporate social responsibility (CSR). Public demands for socially responsible business conduct date back as far as corporations have existed. It was not until around the 1950s, however, that CSR became an academic discipline in its own right and not until the 1960s and 1970s that the topic received widespread academic, business, and media attention. Although the concept has certainly evolved, CSR advocates in the 1960s and 1970s argued that businesspersons should behave like responsible citizens and look beyond their mere economic interests to support and drive social causes, such as fighting poverty, economic disparity, and environmental degradation.[1]

Many traditional, neoclassical economists and management theorists found this trend toward a broad conception of CSR quite troubling. As previously mentioned, Milton Friedman offered a sharp and paradigmatic neoclassical response to the call for a wide sense of CSR. For Friedman and others "there is one and only one social responsibility of business—to use its resources and engage in activities designed to increase its profits so long as it stays within the rules of the game, which is to say, engages in open and free competition without deception or fraud."[2] Friedman thus concludes that managers ought to focus their attention on the needs and expectations of company shareholders and make decisions that best drive corporate profitability. The neoclassical criterion for evaluating strategic management initiatives is certainly clear and managerial performance is readily measurable using standard accounting techniques. Simply put, managers who most efficiently maximize company profits are fulfilling their professional and social responsibilities and nothing more is required; doing more than trying to maximize profits leads to marked inefficiencies and undermines the social values that good businesses promote.

The question becomes, what is the relationship between maximizing profits for shareholders and promoting social welfare? Friedman offers several rather sophisticated arguments that support his position. First, Friedman agrees with the basic utilitarian principle that we should act to try to maximize the greatest good for the greatest number of people. All utilitarians agree to as much. Utilitarians differ, however, on how they define and distinguish between "good" and "bad." Classical utilitarians believe that goodness is synonymous with pleasure and badness with pain. This is not to say, however, that we cannot distinguish between both quantitative and qualitative levels of pleasure and pain. John Stuart Mill, for example, distinguished higher from lower order levels of pleasures.[3] For human beings, higher order levels of pleasure may not be immediately experienced but nevertheless are qualitatively better for those who have experienced them. Having a good education is a typical example of a higher order pleasure and one that we may not appreciate until later in our lives. Conversely, eating a tasty meal will produce pleasure that is qualitatively less than experiencing great art. On the classical account we are thus morally obligated to bring about states of affairs that maximize pleasure or happiness and minimize privation and pain in a more cultivated, but still largely hedonistic sense.

Other utilitarians build on these arguments to argue that what is truly good is the satisfaction of preferences and what is truly bad is the frustration of preferences. Advocates of preference utilitarianism thus claim that one is morally obligated to act if and only if said act best promotes preference satisfaction, which may or may not maximize the most qualitative or quantitative levels of pleasure or sensual experience.

The notion that we ought to maximize happiness and that this is somehow related to preference satisfaction plays an important role in neoclassical analysis. This is a very important point about the neoclassical view, and one that is sometimes overlooked even by its supporters. Friedman and other neoclassical theorists agree that business must provide for the overall social good in order to be justified as legitimate elements of a democratic society, which is to say, that they are not claiming that business is somehow an amoral activity. However, their claim is that the primary way in which businesses contribute to the overall social good is by providing the means by which individuals can best maximize their interests collectively. While the particular details of the theory can be quite complex, there are really two essential elements to the neoclassical argument. The first is that individual preferences, which make up the collective good on this view, are best maximized if people are allowed to pursue their own interests or associate to best pursue shared interests, relatively unrestrained. The second is that managers have an agential and fiduciary obligation to maximize the interests of owners of a company, and that extended attempts to engage in CSR undermine this obligation, and thus fail to both maximize wealth and efficiently distribute resources. We will look at both of these claims in turn.

In the tradition of Adam Smith and preference utilitarians, Friedman thinks that the greatest good is promoted in free and competitive markets where individuals rationally pursue and bargain to fulfill their own preferences. Individual preferences define the good of the individual, and the collective good is merely the sum aggregate of individual goods. Free and competitive markets allow individuals to best fulfill their preferences, since, at least theoretically, such individuals will only engage in exchanges that they believe are to their own benefit (assuming they have perfect information and such transactions are transparent). More simply, in this view people will only engage in those economic transactions that they see as in their own interests, and thus as long as there is no deception or fraud, individual preferences will be maximized overall. This does not mean that there will be no losers in the free market, but it does imply maximized preference satisfaction. Such situations are described as reaching a state of Pareto Efficiency, where the happiness of one person cannot be increased without the happiness of another person being diminished. In other words, any attempt to interfere in basic economic transactions to benefit some other party can only come at the cost of violating the preferences of another and overall utility is reduced.

The managerial role that best aligns with Friedman's vision of the market is clear. In free and competitive markets managers ought to try to most efficiently get products and services into the hands of the consumers that will pay the most for them. This satisfies consumptive consumer preferences. Shareholder interest in exchanging their capital for the promise of maximized return on their investment both reflects and fuels this consumption. And, company profitability captures whether or not a manager is succeeding in this task. It is important to note that for Friedman, successful companies do not merely drive product innovations and satisfy consumer preferences. Successful and profitable companies attract capital that may otherwise leave the market, create and secure jobs and wages, and in turn promote more consumption, provide a tax base for governmental activities and services, and in the end arguably best contribute to overall social welfare. Unsuccessful companies go out of business, thus freeing up any existing capital to be redeployed more efficiently and productively. When all play their respective roles societal preference satisfaction is optimally maximized. The implications of this analysis should not be underestimated. On Friedman's account businesspersons are not merely morally responsible for their own states of affairs. Their actions, omissions, and more generally how they attend to their professional responsibilities impact societal welfare at large.

In this model, extending managerial decision-making beyond company profitability creates more harm than good. Friedman further explains that while we ought to be concerned about and try to eliminate societal ills, such as poverty, crime, and pollution, managers are simply the wrong persons for the job. He points out that managers typically have no training or expertise in dealing with social problems and would simply be inept stewards of social causes. Furthermore, what would likely occur if we demanded that managers champion social causes is that they would opportunistically direct scarce company resources to whatever social causes or charities that are most dear to them. This would not ensure that the most pressing social issues would be efficiently and effectively addressed. This opportunistic behavior would, however, end up increasing agency costs and, while perhaps fulfilling managerial preferences and best intentions, would detract from social wellbeing.[4] The basic point of this view is that managers are not best suited to this task, and that pursuing it would compromise the social obligations for which managers are optimally suited, that is, efficiently pursuing profit. The only acceptable social causes to pursue are those that would provide a return on corporate resources, say through positive marketing, above and beyond other ventures.

Friedman also believes that requiring business managers to champion social causes is socially irresponsible because it undermines the very foundations of a free society. Friedman writes that extending managerial decision-making to help secure social goods beyond profit and wealth is akin to socialism and the "nonsense" spoken in its name "does clearly harm the foundations of a free society."[5] His claim relies on the assumption that there is a direct link between laissez faire oriented free markets and the existence, health, and sustainability of democratic institutions. Undermine the market, and you subvert political freedoms and liberties. In this line of reasoning Friedman is not alone and similar sentiments are echoed by large international institutions, some of the trade liberalization policies of the World Trade Organization included.

It is important to note that Friedman does not, as some charge, think that business and ethics are separate realms or that business ethics is an oxymoron.[6] Indeed, Friedman firmly believes that managers best drive company success by focusing their attention squarely on shareholders and profits and this in turn is objectively good for society. When managers lose sight of this objective they are in fact acting unethically and being socially irresponsible. Further, Friedman specifically claims that businesses ought to avoid fraud and deception and obey the normal moral rules of a society. Perhaps somewhat problematically, Friedman does not greatly expand on what those moral rules are, or why companies are obligated in the preference utilitarian view to be bound by them. The very simplicity of the managerial framework presupposed by the neoclassical view may be its greatest strength, but it also may be belied by the complexities, both theoretical and empirical, that even its proponents seem to acknowledge when discussing the nature and scope of ethical decision-making.

Assessing the Neoclassical Model

Charting the various criticisms and subsequent defenses of neoclassical economics are well beyond the scope of this paper. Some argue in favor of Friedman's laissez faire picture of a free market, others claim that such a view of what a market ought to look like is neither necessary nor sufficient for promoting the greatest good.[7] Some even question the soundness of preference utilitarianism as an indicator of economic and social wellbeing.[8] Philosophically, it is even questionable whether preference utilitarianism can be consistently and coherently defended. Many questions of philosophical psychology, decision modeling, and social identity can also be raised with regard to the theoretical presuppositions made use of in the neoclassical model. While these debates are philosophically interesting, we will focus on a major problem that arises when neoclassical economic theory is used to frame and guide managerial decision-making.

The general observation is that if not in theory, at least in practice, the model leads to a form of managerial myopia where opportunities for value production are lost and risk is increased. One reason for this is that taking profitability for shareholders as the corporate objective function tends to reduce managerial attention to short-term gains, especially when using standard accounting reports and balance sheets or earnings per share calculations.[9] While necessary for managing day-to-day operations, focusing too closely on short-term success does not promote financial sustainability and is not forward looking enough to capture longer term positive and negative trends and opportunities. Strategically and myopically focusing on shareholders, production, and profitability is now seen as a managerial recipe for disaster. This reality poses a distinct problem for new CEOs who tend to regard their function as solely working for the shareholders.[10] Additionally, the focus on short-term gain has been seen by many as responsible for the kinds of extremely poor business decisions that led to the economic crises we have recently experienced in financial markets.

To understand why this would be the case one can consider how short-term profitability can negatively impact production processes. As described in the quality management literature, production processes operate on an input–output basis. For example, marketing departments provide input about customer wants and desires in the form of often quite advanced marketing and behavioral studies. Research and development employees take these inputs and design product specifications that meet these perceived desires. Industrial engineers take these specifications and set up production lines to ensure that products meet the specs. Suppliers provide raw materials that are then transformed per specifications and production plans into products that the customer wants. Shareholder investment and consumer spending on these products provide the necessary capital and cash flow to keep things goings. At each stage of the process inputs are transformed into outputs and value is created, for example, a product that meets customer expectations is defined as a "quality" product. Management systems that efficiently understand and meet customer expectations are quality management systems. Metrics that objectively capture production process performance include such things as on-time delivery, productivity, efficiency and the amount of scrap material produced, and customer satisfaction. Overall processes performance can likewise be captured by various, more encompassing performance measures, including profitability and the more inclusive Balanced Scorecard approach. In general, Balanced Scorecards combine various financial and nonfinancial metrics to create immediate and longer-term value production by investing in a variety of stakeholders and associated processes and metrics.[11]

While we do not necessarily endorse the Balanced Scorecard, we do believe, as most others do, that myopically driving production processes toward rather short-term company profitability goals brings unnecessary risk and can lead to very poor decision-making. A paradigmatic example of this sort of failure is reflected in the hallmark Ford Pinto case. In the 1960s Ford Motor Company executives committed to producing a subcompact car in order to compete with foreign automakers. In order to quickly gain market share Ford accelerated production. In his award winning article "Pinto Madness" Mark Dowie explains what speeding up production means.

> Design, styling, product planning, advance engineering, and quality assurance all have flexible time frames, and engineers can pretty much carry these on simultaneously. Tooling, on the other hand, has a fixed time frame of about 18 months. Normally, an auto company doesn't begin tooling until the other processes are almost over: you don't want to make the machines that stamp and press and grind metal into the shape of car parts until you know all those parts will work well together. *But Iacocca's speed-up meant Pinto tooling went on at the same time as product development.* So when crash tests revealed a serious defect in the gas tank, it was too late. The tooling was well under way.[12]

The defect Dowie alluded to was that with minimal rear-end impact the Pinto would collapse. In many cases this would puncture the gas tank and with a small spark ignite and engulf the car in flames causing death or serious injury Ford knew of such cases and engaged in cost-benefit analysis to guide their decision-making. Estimating 180 burn deaths (at $200,000/death), 180 serious burn injuries (at $67,000/injury), and 2,100 burned cars (at $700/vehicle) the total liability was $49.5 million. Alternatively, to fix the design flaw in all of the affected vehicles would cost $11/vehicle with a total bill of $137 million. In the end Ford's decision backfired and ended up costing the company millions more than initially calculated.[13] The Ford Pinto case is certainly more complex than presented here. Nevertheless, for many their focus on gearing production processes for short-term gain and with it myopic reliance on cost-benefit analysis lead to "ethical fading," where maximizing returns effectively "blinds" good business and ethical decision-making.[14] In the Ford Pinto case, safety was not deemed profitable and thus received little attention in product design, production, and servicing.

Concerning the value of product safety, a very different reaction and outcome is often presented in the case of Johnson & Johnson's voluntary recall of Tylenol aspirin in the early 1980s. A criminal had laced Tylenol capsules with cyanide, which resulted in several deaths. In the wake of these deaths Johnson & Johnson immediately recalled millions of bottles of Tylenol estimated at over $100 million in sales. Citing the company's credo, which dates back to the mid-1940s, Johnson & Johnson executives explained that product safety takes precedence over all other concerns. As explained by Roger Martin of the University of Toronto's Rotman School of Management, for Johnson & Johnson "customers come first, and shareholders last ... (and) when customer satisfaction is at the top of the list shareholders do fine."[15] Johnson & Johnson's long-term outlook is argued to have maximized and sustained company value production. Moving out from specific cases, more extensive empirical data has for some time demonstrated a positive and strong correlation between a company's commitment to ethics and social responsibility (and not just short-term profitability) and financial performance.[16]

While it is certainly the case that employees, suppliers, consumers, and shareholders remain at the center of long-term value production, another problem with myopically focusing on profits and shareholders is that other relationships tend to be regarded as external to organizational performance. More recent work in stakeholder management rightfully views all relationships with a company as possibly contributing to or detracting from company success. In stakeholder management literature and practice, business is a more accurately described as a very complex and embedded social activity involving numerous, extended relationships with communities, media outlets, governments, political groups, activists, trade associations, unions, and other constituencies. As stakeholders are potentially impacted by and impact company success, all of these relationships warrant managerial attention. Note that this does not mean that stakeholders deserve equal treatment, merely equal consideration. Understanding and being equally responsive to stakeholders opens up new opportunities for value creation, helps to identify risks, and makes a company more cognizant of and adaptable to changing market conditions.[17]

In this vein, thinking of managers as mere agents for shareholders and characterizing them as opportunistic and inept custodians of the social good limits company success. While managers and other businesspersons may not have the experience and training to successfully deal with some social problems, such as crime, poverty, and inflation, they are certainly in a position to best advance other social objectives. Indeed, it is now generally recognized that entrepreneurially oriented businesses are often in the best position to address important social issues, and, in doing so, to create value for their own company. This does not mean that managers have the expertise to positively deal with all or any social problems. Neither does it mean, however, that managers are inept, especially when engaging community, nongovernmental, or not-for-profit organizational stakeholders in public–private partnerships.

Although maligned in the business ethics literature for their handling of the Pinto case, Ford Motor Company's current actions serve as a benchmark for how to effectively and efficiently champion social causes and likewise drive company success in ways that are certainly not inept. Calling on the words of their founder, Henry Ford, the current ethos at Ford recognizes that "A business that makes nothing but money is a poor business." Additionally, CEO Alan Mulally declares that despite the challenging economic times he has "never lost sight of the environmental and the social goals that are key elements of our business strategy. Indeed, our focus on those goals was an important factor in our financial recovery. By delivering cars that are greener, safer, and smarter, we enhanced our competitiveness and built stronger relationships with our customers." Stemming from this commitment to environmental and social goals, some of the causes that Ford champions are philanthropic in nature and motivate increased employee participation in programs such as Ford Global Week of Caring and community building projects. Furthermore the Ford Dreams through Education Fund and the League of United Latin American Citizens have teamed up to address dropout rates among Latino students across the country. In addition to more philanthropic initiatives, Ford endeavors to promote social causes in their industry. To this end Ford leverages their position as an OEM to work with suppliers, competitors, and nonprofit organizations to make a positive impact in the markets in which they do business. Specific efforts include requiring supplier compliance with the environmental standard ISO 14000. It also includes working with the Automotive Industry Action Group to promote environmental sustainability and human rights in the Middle East, Mexico, and South America.[18]

Of course, Ford is not alone in this area. Many other companies are proving that doing well as a company and doing what is good are not only compatible but in many ways mutually dependent. Sustainability expert Chris Laszlo documents similar success stories at such companies as DuPont, Lafarge, NatureWorks LLC, and even Wal-Mart.[19] We also find similar movements in the highly criticized US banking industry where financial institutions are beginning to champion sometimes quite advanced and innovative financial literacy programs, often in underprivileged communities. Capital One, for example, is engaged in a public–private partnership with the nonprofit group Consumer Action. Together they have launched MoneyWise, which provides free multilingual financial educational material and curriculum. Additionally, Capital One has set up and supervises student run banks in the Bronx, Newark, and Harlem to help teach students banking and other money management skills.[20]

Given these and other examples, Friedman's inept custodian argument simply does not hold water. While businesses should not champion each and every social cause, they most certainly can offer advice and direction that is within their area of expertise. So, more specifically, Friedman commits the fallacy of overgeneralization, by moving from a limited and narrow set of social problems, such as crime, poverty, and inflation, to a universal conclusion about managerial competence.[21]

The fact that managers and their companies have and continually do successfully champion social causes also undercuts Friedman's doom and gloom "free society" argument. We have witnessed a variety of corporate social initiatives without losing our democratic liberties and rights. We have likewise found relatively free markets operating for long periods of time within repressive and antidemocratic political regimes. As such, the relationship between markets, economics, and political institutions is certainly a very complex matter, but there is no real fear that extending managerial attention to include social responsibilities beyond shareholders and profitability would undermine free society scholars note that Friedman's free society argument constitutes a fallacious appeal to emotions.[22]

Finally, we should remember that the limited liability corporation itself is a social construct, and not a natural kind. This fact is often overlooked in the neoclassical literature which seems to ignore the fact that governments grant special privileges to shareholders not possessed by other property owners (mainly those of limited liability), precisely to encourage desired social ends (the investment of capital, etc.). Since limited liability itself is a kind of social bargain struck between democratic governments and investors, there should be every expectation that corporations, in turn, can have obligations and duties not possessed by other agents. That is to say, if corporations fail to serve a larger social purpose and contribute to the general good in specifically defined ways, there is no reason to think they should continue to be granted the special privileges that they are.

Certainly, the US Supreme Court's decision regarding *Citizens United* and other decisions tend to recognize corporations as legal persons and thus they must be granted the rights that all persons are afforded, such as due process and freedom of speech. While this is philosophically contentious and we think metaphysically unsound (corporations appear to be nothing more than a collection of extant contracts), recognizing companies as persons should bolster our case. After all, we at least require persons to be *Minimally Good Samaritans.* That is, when persons are in a position to promote a great good or to prevent a great harm without incurring too much risk or expending too many resources, we think that they are morally obligated to do so. If a person, a good swimmer in their own right, is walking by a pool and sees a child drowning and decides not to save the child because they will then miss a hairstyling appointment, we would rightly regard them as exceedingly immoral and perhaps in some cases legally culpable. The child may not have a right to be saved but failing to do so is nevertheless morally reprehensible. In our view, corporations as persons would be morally obligated to do what is good in similar and analogous circumstances (industrially polluted environments disproportionally affect poor children).

Aside from ascribing normative commitments on the basis of the Minimally Good Samaritan basis, one could agree with much of what Friedman claims holds true on utilitarian grounds, but regard his argument as unsound nonetheless. One could agree that we ought to promote the greatest good for the greatest number of people and that a free and competitive market is the best economic system for maximizing overall happiness. One could also agree that company success in such a system best promotes social welfare. One could even argue, as we will in chapter 2, that the manager–shareholder relationship creates very strong and fundamental managerial obligations to attend to shareholder needs and expectations. Despite all of this, the neoclassical, shareholder centric, and profit-oriented managerial framework simply does not best promote and capture organizational success and failure. As it fails on descriptive and instrumental or strategic grounds it likewise fails within a utilitarian, normative framework.

Perhaps setting up Friedman's somewhat dated arguments in this way is a bit unfair. Indeed, even those who maintain a shareholder, wealth or value-oriented conception of the corporate objective function, now reject profitability for shareholders as a sound management perspective. Michael Jensen, for example, argues against the Balanced Scorecard approach, but recognizes that "short-term profit maximization at the expense of long-term value creation is a sure way to destroy value."[23]

This is where "enlightened" stakeholder theory can play an important role. We can learn from stakeholder theorists how to lead managers and participants in an organization to think more generally and creatively about how the organization's policies treat all important constituencies of the firm. This includes not just the stockholders and financial markets, but employees, customers, suppliers, and the community in which the organization exists. Indeed, it is a basic principle of enlightened value maximization that we cannot maximize the long-term market value of an organization if we ignore or mistreat any important constituency.[24] For authors like Jensen, profitability is giving way to such longer-term financial metrics as Economic Value Added, Market Value Added, Total Market Value, Total Shareholder Return, and Shareholder Value Creation.

Thus adopting the neoclassical economic model as a basis ethical–organizational integrity is ill conceived, even if financial success remains the primary corporate objective. So like many others, we think that stakeholder management is better justified on descriptive, strategic, and normative grounds and provides a superior framework for understanding, grounding, and promoting ethical–organizational integrity.[25] We now need to look more closely at what the more enlightened stakeholder management framework requires us to do.

Doing Good—Stakeholder Management

The stakeholder management concept dates back at least to Standard Oil Chairman of the Board Frank Abrams' appeal to shareholders that managers ought to be equally responsible for supporting the interests of stockholders, employees, customers, communities, and the public at large.[26] Additional developments in the stakeholder concept occurred with the development of Russell Ackoff's systems approach to management and William Dill's participatory approach to management.[27] The notion of stakeholder management was formalized in the 1980s by RE Freeman with his groundbreaking work on how and why managers ought to identify and align the interests of a wide range of individuals and groups previously regarded as external to managerial purview.[28] Since then, stakeholder theorists have overcome some rather entrenched criticisms, including claims that stakeholder management is anticapitalistic, cannot provide an objective corporate function, and provides an excuse for managerial opportunism.[29] Now, the term "stakeholder" is an accepted part of the organizational management vernacular in one form or another.

Two major reasons for this acceptance are as follows. First, effective stakeholder management is now seen as essential for long term company value production and success. William George frames it best when stating "Serving all your stakeholders is the best way to product long-term results and create a growing, prosperous company … there is no conflict between servicing all your stakeholders and providing excellent returns for shareholders. In the long term it is impossible to have one without the other."[43] Correlatively, effective stakeholder management is now seen as necessary for maximizing and sustaining overall social welfare, e.g., by promoting environmental and social responsibility or otherwise producing the best consequences for all involved. These points are further drawn out and substantiated later in this chapter.

This of course does not mean that all stakeholder management issues have been resolved. The thousands of books and articles devoted to the topic evidence this fact. For example, there are debates about the proper normative foundations of stakeholder management. The literature in this area is as diverse as in moral philosophy itself and virtue,[30] Kantian,[31] care,[32] discourse ethical,[33] pragmatic,[34] Rawlsian,[35] libertarian,[36] and other theoretical approaches abound. There continues to be considerable discussion about proper stakeholder identification and salience.[37] Questions regarding the relationship between fiduciary obligations and stakeholder management are still being raised.[38] There are also of course various opinions on how to best measure managerial performance.[39] Some, like Jensen, think that company success is synonymous with long-term wealth production. Some think that corporations should be held to a triple bottom line, reflecting financial, environmental, and social performance, and some argue for the Balanced Scorecard approach. And, although Freeman does not claim to advocate any particular corporate objective function, he does claim that managers ought to try to maximize value for all stakeholders. Other sources are much better suited to provide a more comprehensive treatment of the history of the stakeholder concept and related theoretical and practical issues, but it is worthwhile to note the wide range of variants, issues, and debates surrounding stakeholder theory.[40]

As mentioned in the introduction, we do not claim to resolve all theoretical and practical issues and we do not believe that there is one fixed stakeholder management approach that does so. To our mind, stakeholder theory is better thought of as a heuristic model, or "narrative" in Freeman's account, meant to guide practical decision-making, than as a complete theoretical formulation.[41] We believe it provides a metaphor and a model for managers to think about the various normative and empirical factors relevant to practical decision-making, and does so in a way that is better than the alternative models. While not intended as a theoretically complete account of or an algorithm for decision-making, we do believe that it provides a paradigm for the kind of informed and deliberative decision-making that Aristotle referred to as practical wisdom.[42] In short, one's particular industry, level of economic performance, company, and existing organizational culture will determine the details that fit your situation. What we will offer are some general, guiding stakeholder management strategies that will conceptually ground more specific stakeholder oriented, ethical–organizational integrity efforts.

The first strategy for effective stakeholder management begins with properly identifying company stakeholders. In the most general sense, we define stakeholders as any individual or group whose claim on a firm's activities could promote or inhibit company value creation and ultimately company success. This aligns with other broad definitions and entails that a wide range of potential stakeholders will exist for any corporation; including, but not limited to, shareholders and other financers, customers, employees, suppliers, competitors, governments and citizens, and various community members and groups, under which we will include local and global communities, activist and advocacy groups, nongovernmental organizations, and the media. Figure 1.1 provides a simple depiction of a wide set of company stakeholders.

Figure 1.1 is perhaps oversimplified, as understanding general stakeholder categories is too abstract to be useful. Within each category managers must identify the specific stakeholders with which they are distinctly related. As mentioned above the category of "community" holds various constituencies. Additionally, there are various types and levels of employees ranging from executives to types of nonexempt workers. Some shareholders have long-term commitments to a firm and others may be short-term traders and some shareholder groups are more powerful than

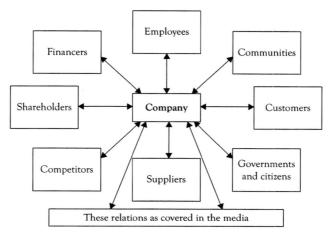

Figure 1.1. A wide stakeholder view of the firm.

others. Furthermore, it should be noted that relations with each stakeholder constituency can be of interest to the media (they may not have a claim on a firm's activities but may certainly have an interest in a firm's decisions) and lead to either positive or negative publicity. Thus within each stakeholder category there are often various types of constituencies that make different sorts of specific claims on a firm.

These claims can and often are economic and transactional in nature. Employees exchange their labor and issue a claim with regards to wages. Suppliers exchange products or services for payment. Shareholders certainly claim a financial return on their investment. There are also claims that are more explicitly moral or ethical in nature. For example, an employee may claim to deserve a "living" wage in exchange for their labor or desire meaningful work. Community members may lay rightful claim to their cultural heritage and integrity and demand that certain organizational activities that infringe upon their established way of life be stopped. Activist groups may claim that organizational activities that lead to environmental degradation or global warming are unjust. The implications of looking beyond a transactional and purely economic understanding of relationships will further play out in chapter 3 when we briefly discuss leadership models. The point to make here is that stakeholders hold claims that cannot and ought not to be merely negotiated away by mere economic incentives or threats. Furthermore, we explain in chapter 2 that some stakeholder claims are morally supported by very weighty fundamental rights that ought always to be respected. For example, an employee's right to freedom of movement (whether they claim such a right or not) ought never to be denied, for example, chaining a worker to a machine is never morally acceptable. In any event, the second step is to fill in the wide stakeholder categories with particular stakeholder groups and then to identify the specific claims each group is making.

In terms of these stakeholder claims, managers should understand that in principle the ability to effectively address and meet stakeholder expectations is valuable and processes should be established to do so (more on what these processes should look like in chapter 3). In terms of financial expectations this is quite easy to understand. Failing to meet employee salary demands may undercut employee retention rates. Failing to pay suppliers on time may lead to poor quality. Additionally, continually failing to pay out shareholder dividends may limit capital investments. All three examples would impact company success and compromise long-term value production. In addition to meeting financial claims, there is also opportunity to promote value and company success by understanding and meeting ethical claims. The notion of social capital can be used to explain this point. At its basis the concept of social capital is a simple one. As Francis Fukuyama explains, social capital is "a capability that arises from the prevalence of trust in a society or in certain parts of it … if people who have to work together in an enterprise trust one another because they are all operating according to a common set of ethical norms, doing business costs less."[44] Thus doing what is perceivably good for stakeholders (addressing and trying to meet their financial and nonfinancial claims) opens up opportunities for sustainable value creation and drives company success. Although certainly not exhaustive, Table 1.1 addresses some stakeholder claims and areas for potential and measurable value creation.

So, the first stakeholder strategy is to identify stakeholders and the claims they make, understanding the potential for short- and long-term value creation when said claims are met. While setting up processes to identify and try to fulfill stakeholder claims is important, it is also important to understand that potential for value creation may not be explicitly expressed as a claim. In many cases persons or organizations may not

Table 1.1. *Stakeholder Claims and Value Creation and Destruction*

Stakeholder	Types of claims	Potential for value creation
Shareholders	Fair return on investment Transparency Truthful financial reporting Regulatory compliance More democratic governance	Increases capital investment, decreases the cost of capital, contributes to more effective and efficient corporate governance, positive media coverage
Employees (at various levels of the company)	Respect Fair wages Equal treatment and nondiscrimination Healthy and safe working conditions Job security Participation Due process Meaningful work Privacy	Increases employee productivity, efficiency, and quality, helps a company attract and keep top talent, creates a dynamic and innovative workplace, promotes human and intellectual capital, positive media coverage
Customers	Quality products Product safety Truth in sales and advertising Social and environmental responsibility Management system standardization	Increases customer retention and brand loyalty, inspires customer trust, "going green" and being ethical is good marketing, management system quality and environmental standardization increases company efficiency, capability, and capacity, positive media coverage

(Continued)

Table 1.1. Stakeholder Claims and Value Creation and Destruction—(Continued)

Suppliers	Fair procurement practices On-time payment for services Workable lead times Management system help (e.g., implementing environmental and social accountability organizational standards) Technology and knowledge investment	Contributes to lean manufacturing, inventory optimization, responsiveness to customer and market changes, promotes human and intellectual, positive media coverage
Communities (e.g., non-governmental organizations, local and global community groups, activists, etc.)	Economic development Philanthropy Corporate social responsibility Environmental responsibility	Leads to good public and media relations, creates mutually beneficial public–private relationships, promotes human and intellectual capital, prevents activist group intervention, positive media coverage
Government(s) and their citizens	Regulatory compliance Ethics and compliance systems Environmental and social responsibility	Helps to reduce compliance costs and the costs of unethical and/or illegal conduct, improves public reputation, positive media coverage
Competitors	Fair play Compliance with anti-trust and corporate laws	Decrease costs of compliance and illegal activity, helps promote industries that customer, employees, and other stakeholders can trust, positive media coverage

be in a position to express that which is truly best for them and in turn for one's company. For example, company suppliers may not explicitly desire to design and implement a formal quality management system, but doing might significantly improve product quality, cut production costs, increase customer satisfaction, and even give them a competitive advantage over other suppliers. Employees working in impoverished areas may be satisfied with a low wage and voice no other concerns. But improving work place health and safety or educating employees will often improve their situation and boost company performance. To cite another example, a company's board of directors may be for whatever reason disposed (sometimes out of ignorance) to focus on short-term company profitability. Helping them to understand more sophisticated financial and long-term performance metrics and strategies would enable them to make better financial decisions. As members of the US based, National Association of Corporate Directors, companies like Aetna, the Home Depot, and McDonald's encourage board development in these and other areas.[45] In short, simply trying to satisfy stakeholder preferences would thus leave opportunities for value creation unrealized.

The second stakeholder strategy is to do good by trying to promote mutual stakeholder capabilities or, in other words, to do good by improving on what a stakeholder can achieve (e.g., through education, training, improvements in quality of life) in order to generate valuable outcomes and mutually drive company success. General or potential stakeholders were defined as any individual or group whose relationship provides opportunities for value creation or destruction or who may positively or negatively impact value and company success. We define mutual stakeholders as having a shared or joint interest in company success, such that developing their capabilities (e.g., for rational decision-making) helps to drive and sustain company success. Mutual stakeholders tend to include shareholders, employees, suppliers, consumers, and some members of one's community. Some community activist groups, for example, work with companies to create better communities, while others may desire to undermine company endeavors. Competitors can be mutual stakeholders, but typically only in the case of a joint project or under the guise of an industry association.

As was the case in analyzing stakeholder claims, it is equally important to note that developing capabilities requires more than economic incentives and often involves protecting and promoting the basic things required for living a fuller and more meaningful life. The work of Martha Nussbaum and Amartya Sen illustrates and support these facts.[46] Again, the relationship between business and ethics is further strengthened. While the work of Nussbaum and Sen tends to be set at the macro-economic level, their ideas readily translate into strategies for organizational success. Table 1.2 lists some of the general principles, rationale, and related applications for promoting stakeholder capabilities in the workplace, down supply chains, and across industries and communities.[47]

As already mentioned Ford Motor Company works to promote supplier and even competitor capabilities in terms of promoting environmental sustainability and human rights. With regard to environmental sustainability Ford actively works with suppliers and industry partners to encourage the development and implementation of environmental management systems, life-cycle product and tooling analysis, environmental modeling, and various other sustainability management tools. Concerning human rights issues, Ford and other companies have worked with governments, suppliers, and industry partners to develop, implement, and enforce standardized codes for acceptable labor practices. Ford Motor Company's Code of Basic Working Conditions is included in Appendix A.

Additionally, Capital One tries to promote the financial literacy of its customers and community members. In addition to promoting environmental sustainability, Deutsche Bank makes social investments in promoting community arts and music and educational programs and even issuing loans with the explicit purpose of improving the quality of life and opportunities for those in impoverished areas. Efforts to promote stakeholder capabilities are also undertaken in the public sector. The Australian Public Service Commission (APSC) recognize that capability building is central to organizational performance and produced detailed guidelines for promoting the learning and development of public sector employees. Their efforts centered on the principles illustrated in Figure 1.2 (a more detailed checklist offered by the APSC is included in Appendix B).[50]

The two strategies for effective stakeholder management and doing what is good in business are to (1) do what is good for stakeholders by understanding and meeting their claims and (2) do what is good for

Table 1.2. Promoting Mutual Stakeholder Capabilities

Principle	Explanation	Some applications
Develop a shared affiliation in a higher cause	People are more motivated to perform their job when the value of their performance extends beyond material gain	Be clear about the importance of ethics, integrity, and social responsibility and include mutual stakeholders when forming and carrying out ethics based initiatives.[48] Extend ethics based initiatives and commitments to "higher causes" down the organizational supply chain.
Promote physical and emotional wellbeing and security	Working in a healthy and safe workplace increases productivity and efficiency	Establish procedures, incentives, and controls and work with communities and supply chains to eliminate physical and mental abuse and create environments that respect and promote bodily and emotional integrity.
Foster imagination, innovation, and free thought	Creative environments foster product and process innovations	Include mutual stakeholders in planning, brainstorming, and continual improvement activities. Respect freedom of speech and association and limit paternalistic involvement.
Develop practical reasoning skills and promote education	Developing critical thinking and promoting education are main drivers of human and intellectual capital	Encourage and reward employee educational advancements. Build a better resource base by investing in community education programs, for example, fiscal literacy. Help promote supply chain organizational advancements. Ensure that consumers have all of the relevant information to make an informed choice.
Foster constructive play	Play is a critical and positive feature of organizational culture; play encourages employee satisfaction, retention; play can lead to innovation	Work and play are not mutually exclusive. Find ways to combine work activities and task with play and leisure activities. Create free spaces where creative innovation is encouraged. Create collaborative virtual environments that combine work, play, and shared problem solving.[49] Encourage team-building play activities.

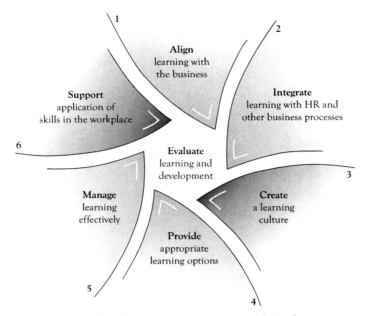

Figure 1.2. Principles for promoting learning and development.

mutual stakeholders by developing their capabilities. Obviously, a company and its managers cannot meet every claim and develop all capabilities and choices need to be made. Deciding between competing choices and stakeholder demands brings with it the potential for conflict. When doing so keep the following suggestions in mind. First, do not ignore a stakeholder group and be sure to take some action in terms of (1) and (2). Do not fall into "either–or" decision-making, for example, either we meet our shareholder claims or our employee claims. Second, prioritize claims and capabilities with regard to the potential for short- and long-term value production and competitive advantage. Tie your expectations into standard and more advanced financial metrics and process oriented objectives (more on this in chapter 3). Remember that in principle doing what is good for stakeholders promotes company success and at the same time more positively promotes ethical, social, and environmental responsibility initiatives. Third, think creatively and entrepreneurially about how to meet claims and develop capabilities. Look to best-in-practices benchmarks for guidance. Fourth, establish processes to ensure continual improvement (again, more on this in chapter 3) and make sure that your

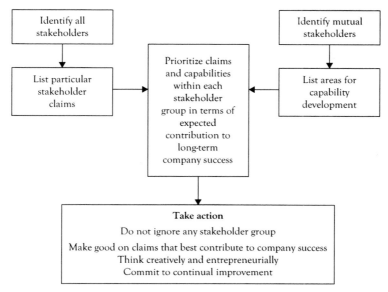

Figure 1.3. Doing what is good for stakeholders.

stakeholders know company actions are taken for their benefit. Even if all claims cannot be met and all capabilities developed, doing these four things will help to maintain personal and organizational identity when there is conflict or limited resources. Figure 1.3 represents the basics of doing what is good for stakeholders.

Conclusion

In the past stakeholder management was criticized on several grounds. A detailed analysis of these criticisms can be found elsewhere.[51] Some have argued that stakeholder management cannot provide a clear and measurable corporate objective function and this in turn will lead to managerial opportunism. In our model, managerial opportunism can be controlled by objectively calculating the degree to which managerial decision-making contributes to long-term valuation and competitive advantage (collectively comprising company success). While we do not take a stand on what system of measurement one ought to use, many are available and objective enough to evaluate managerial performance. Stakeholder initiatives as suggested in this chapter can be tied to various standard (e.g., quality metrics) and emerging performance metrics (e.g., social and environmental capital). Others have argued that stakeholder management implies that all stakeholders must be treated equally. We agree that stakeholders and their claims demand equal consideration, as all stakeholders can impact value production. Equal consideration, however, does not imply equal treatment. All things being equal and where no stakeholder group is wholly ignored, managers ought to attend to stakeholder claims and develop mutual capabilities that better drive sustainable company success.

Finally, a number of critics have suggested that stakeholder management requires particular, often democratic or even socialistic, organizational structures and forms of corporate governance. We, and others, realize that stakeholder management is less a theory and more a flexible hermeneutic or heuristic to describe, interpret, narrate, and explain business relationships. As such, we follow Freeman to the extent we believe that stakeholder management permits and endorses the formulation and evaluation of many organizational structures; indeed, the more narratives the better.[52] Some companies may benefit by traditional, hierarchical models, others may benefit by open book management styles, and even others by blended forms of corporate governance. As not all companies and organizational cultures are the same, within the stakeholder framework, capable managers will explore various organizational narratives and implement those that work best. In this sense, trying to do what is good for stakeholders and concomitantly trying to drive long-term company success is an entrepreneurial process that requires open, dynamic, and innovative leaders.

In the introduction we mentioned ethical–organizational integrity involves doing that which is good. That being said, figuring out exactly what ethics requires can be difficult. While we can agree that managers ought to promote that which is good for their company and overall social welfare, exactly how this should be accomplished is open to much debate. In the neoclassical managerial model, managers are said to do what is good by trying to maximize profits for shareholders. While we agree in principle that in largely free and competitive markets company success does in fact best promote overall social welfare, we also argued that the neoclassical managerial model is too myopic, misses opportunities for value creation, and unduly jeopardizes company health and overall social well being. Alternatively, the stakeholder management framework is a far better model for doing what is good in business and for society, which includes meeting financial and ethical claims, developing capabilities, and exhibiting social and environmental responsibility.

In the next chapter we will look more closely at the nature of stakeholder claims in light of doing what is right. We will learn that on the basis of certain stakeholder holder rights, in the name of doing what is good there are things that we always morally obligated to do and things that we are morally obligated never to do.

Questions for Further Inquiry

What are some of the philosophical critiques of free market economics?

What are some of the normative disputes in stakeholder management?

What are some of the controversies regarding stakeholder identification and salience?

Should companies adopt a Balanced Scorecard approach or singular value calculation metric?

Is there anything wrong with adopting a triple-bottom-line (3BL)?

What are some of the best-in-practice CSR initiatives?

Do CSR obligations differ from country to country? Are any legally mandated?

What are some of the common pitfalls associated with CSR initiatives?

CHAPTER 2

Rights, Duties, and Other Obligations

In the last chapter we stated that one essential aspect for promoting ethical–organizational integrity is trying to do what is good for stakeholders. More specifically, doing what is good means understanding and trying to meet stakeholder expectations and developing mutual stakeholder capabilities. When done well this is best for one's career, company, and society. In this chapter, we introduce a second essential component for promoting ethical–organizational integrity. This involves understanding and doing what is right. What we will soon realize is that while managing for stakeholders and driving company success is good, certain attempts to do so may violate important rights and thus may not be morally justified. For example, the use of exploited child labor ought never to be seen as a legitimate value driver. In the most basic sense, all managerial theories acknowledge a duty on the part of management to do what is right, which at times could conflict with that which is perceived as good. However, theories disagree over what the concept of rightness includes.

In the first section of this chapter, we illustrate this disagreement by first examining the neoclassical theory of the firm and how it defines proper moral conduct. As we explain, in the neoclassical model a manager largely discharges the obligation to do the right thing by acting as a good agent, respecting shareholder rights, and meeting minimal standards of morality. We argue that this view is too myopic and morally unjustified. As was the case in our examination of doing what is good, we and others think that stakeholder management provides a more useful decision-making framework, in this case for identifying and prioritizing various rights and corresponding obligations. The second section of the chapter explains important rights-based terminology, which, although somewhat technical, will help students and managers work through those difficult situations when rights and other obligations seem to conflict. Having a firm philosophical framework for understanding rights will help in this endeavor. We then outline some of the prominent rights held by organizational stakeholders and corresponding managerial duties and obligations.

The Neoclassic Account of Doing Right

In the last chapter we argued that the neoclassical model fails to do what is best for company success and overall social welfare. Independent of consequences, however, proponents try to conclude that managers are obligated to maximize profits for shareholders by appealing to rights. Again, we'll take Milton Friedman's analysis as representative of the neoclassical position and briefly outline his arguments. Friedman explains that shareholders are citizens and already pay income taxes to the government, which include profits from equity investments. These taxes are collected and freely elected representatives can use these monies to promote certain social goods and programs. Extending managerial responsibility to include additional social welfare programs is unfair on principle because it amounts to a form of taxation without representation. Shareholders turn over their private capital to managerial agents with the explicit purpose of maximizing the return on their investment. In devoting time and resources to pursuing their own social objectives managers are in effect spending someone else's money. Friedman maintains that such actions violate shareholder proprietary rights and fail to fulfill a manager's agential and fiduciary responsibility to place their principal's interests ahead of all others. Summarizing Friedman's claims, moving corporate social responsibility beyond profits is on principle wrong because it would violate shareholder constitutional, proprietary, and fiduciary rights.[1]

Like his consequentialist based analysis, Friedman's rights based arguments are also problematic and prove to be unsound. Specifically, the claims that devoting company resources to social and ethical objectives is tantamount to taxation without representation and violates fiduciary duties and proprietary rights lose their force when we reframe the argument using the proper terminology. Following a long tradition of organizational management theory, managers do not impose taxes on shareholders, but rather make expenditures that show up as financial liabilities or costs. And, there is nothing unethical or illegal on principle about increasing liabilities or adding costs. In fact, increasing financial liabilities or imposing operating costs without direct shareholder approval is an accepted, necessary, and desired managerial function. Managers are paid to use their training and expertise to allocate resources on a discretionary basis.

Friedman is correct to say, however, that it is unethical to violate a manager's fiduciary obligations to shareholders. Shareholders turn over capital with the faith and trust that managers will direct their investments in order to best drive company success and thus promote a healthy return on their investment. Fiduciary obligations are specifically designed to prevent the opportunistic exploitation of this trust. As such, managers must maintain transparency, engage in truthful reporting, try to best carry out the duties and nominal functions covered in their job description, and eliminate or disclose conflicts of interest. Additionally, managers are not allowed to take monetary gain at the expense of company success. In short, managers put shareholder interests first by placing company success first and honestly reporting on the financial status of the firm. Correlatively, shareholders own their financial stake in a firm and may exit the relationship or exert their influence through a company's defined governance structure if they do not think executives are meeting performance expectations.

Yet, while shareholders are entitled certain rights, their claims on managerial behavior are not proprietary in nature. Shareholders own their stock, but do not necessarily own the company in which they invest, at least in the same sense that shareholders and other persons possess their own personal property. For example, shareholders do not exercise direct control over company assets. Of course, shareholders do have a right to company earnings, but on the whole their influence on a firm is indirect. Shareholders can try to influence company decision-making vis-à-vis the threat of exit or by influencing the company's board of directors. As recognized by some, Friedman's proprietary based argument for shareholder primacy is seen to be his weakest.[2] This, of course, is not meant to suggest that shareholders as investors (particularly investors that are in a relationship of acute vulnerability and dependence and whose trust is necessary to have a functioning market) ought not to be granted special moral considerations. It merely suggests that it is misleading to think that special moral considerations stem from firm ownership.

Thus, imposing costs that represent good faith attempts to drive company success simply does not constitute opportunistic exploitation, does not violate shareholder proprietary rights, and does not amount to a form of taxation without representation.[3]

Additionally, in the same way that myopically focusing organization metrics and strategies on driving profitability or even value for shareholders closes off opportunities for value creation, the same case can be made in the case of rights. That is, in the worst cases myopically focusing on shareholders closes off the consideration of prima facie rights from other stakeholder constituencies, including employees, suppliers, consumers, and communities.[4] As we will learn, these rights include entitlements as fundamental as human rights. The Ford Pinto case is an example where a corporate culture focused on short-term profitability limited the consideration of rather basic consumer rights to know the safety risks of unreasonably dangerous vehicles.

As was the case when trying to understand obligations to do what is good, a stakeholder oriented approach to rights provides a more inclusive and helpful managerial framework for recognizing important rights and correlative duties. The next section provides some rights-based terminology that will help managers better understand the nature and extent of stakeholder rights and deal with moral conflict.

Rights-Based Terminology

While focusing primarily on shareholder rights will not do, expanding managerial vision to better consider a larger set of stakeholder rights can be difficult. Indeed, the very simplicity of the neoclassical model of managerial obligation may in large part explain its pragmatic appeal. Moving beyond the neoclassical model necessitates acknowledging a diversity of potential obligations that managers must face and integrate into their decision-making. As even many people who agree with the critique of the neoclassical model recognize, providing for managerial principles that do so complicates the nature of managerial decision-making.[5] However, in our view this difficulty should not be overemphasized. Indeed, we believe that a clear focus on the basic notion of rights is the best way to illuminate the proper scope and nature of managerial obligations. Defining some key rights-based terms will help make this transition easier, and so we turn to this task first.

In the most general sense a right is simply an entitlement to act in a certain way (or not to act in a certain way) and/or to be treated in a certain manner. That is to say, if a person has a right to free speech, then that person is entitled to speak freely if they so choose. Likewise, if a person has a right to some money owed to her, then she is entitled to be paid back. Importantly, every right entails a duty or obligation on the part of other persons. So, to use the examples above again, if a person has a right to free speech, then others have a duty not to suppress his speech and if a person has a right to some money owed to her, then someone else has an obligation to pay her the money back. Of course, many of our rights and duties are codified in law. In business, shareholder rights and managerial obligations are laid down in securities regulations. Employee rights to a healthy and safe workplace are defined in occupational health and safety mandates. Consumers are protected by product liability laws and truth in advertising regulations and rights protecting competitors are laid out in corporate and antitrust law. Additionally, rights and duties are tied to various professional roles and spelled out in various codes of ethical conduct.

Rights can be generated from many different kinds of, and often overlapping sources. It is thus is important to distinguish between legal and political rights, as well as professional rights and moral rights when talking about rights in a business context. Legal and political rights and duties are grounded in existing laws and practices and tend to focus upon issues of compliance. Often legal duties are taken to represent the minimal obligations that companies have to respect. Some of the more significant protections occur under the guise of civil rights. Civil rights tend to legally protect groups from discrimination and promote equality and equal opportunity. Legislation tends to protect employment discrimination on the basis of age, gender, religion, race, national origin, and increasingly sexual preference and gender identity. These sorts of rights are codified in the US Bill of Rights, various European Union Treaties, the UN Declaration on Human Rights, and the International Covenant on Civil and Political Rights. Other legal rights and corresponding duties regarding corporate conduct are reflected in various levels of national and international corporate law, regarding such things as corruption, antitrust, environmental responsibilities, health and safety, sales and marketing, and product safety.

In addition to rights and duties codified in law, some rights and duties arise from our voluntary associations and relationships. For example, professional rights and obligations generally stem from the consensus of an established body of experts in a field and typically represent the considered view of that body as to what those professionals and their stakeholders are entitled to in the practice of the profession. Additionally, organizations may and ought to define their ethical expectations and correlative rights and duties. Generally such professional and organizational rights are codified in some manner and some provisions are provided for maintaining professional or organizational adherence to their strictures. For instance, while a failure of professional obligation may not result in a legal claim against a professional, it might still result in a professional sanction of some kind, such as loss of certification. Failing to meet an ethical–organizational expectation may result in demotion or termination. While professional and organizational obligations are generally less fully integrated into the judicial system as legal obligations, there is often an overlap between these obligations in practice (for instance, professional boards may be given the legal authority to govern certain aspects of professional practice in some fields). For example, when joining the Sales and Marketing Executives International organization, members are expected to acquiesce to the rules of ethical conduct (see Appendix C). Other professional associations, including associations of accountants, lenders, mortgage realtors, engineers, journalists, information technologists, computer programmers, and others, adhere to their own ethical codes. These codes often extend beyond the letter of the law and expect more than mere compliance. Other voluntary obligations arise at more personal levels. For example, if I agree to give you a ride home after work you have a right to expect me to do so.

Finally, moral rights are generated out of particular moral systems and may or may not carry any sort of official sanction or be generally recognized in any substantial manner. While many legal, political, and professional rights stem from and reflect certain concepts of moral rights, it is nonetheless true that at least some (and in some areas many) of what are typically referred to as moral rights and duties may not be codified in law, or professional affiliation. For example, libertarian oriented moral rights entitle all human beings to liberty and property. All governments and political structures, however, do not reflect these rights. Accordingly, moral rights and duties provide a basis for a more robust normative evaluation of actions and practices. The types of rights commonly discussed in business are identified in Table 2.1.

Of course, the difficulty with claims about moral rights and obligations is that there is no generally accepted agreement on what moral system should be universally adopted. Not surprisingly, both ordinary people and philosophers have often held lots of different views about what the correct moral system is. Nonetheless, we should not let such disagreement lead us to question the general significance of rights. Indeed, what is perhaps more informative than the disagreements is what these different theories can tell us about the importance of rights. In this regard, we would accent that while there is no philosophical agreement as to what moral system we should adopt, there is general agreement about the importance of moral rights and duties. Moral claims, at both the practical and theoretical level, are rife with talk about rights, and nearly every theory acknowledges that we have to account for the significance of this language of rights and duties in some manner. Second, we would note that looking at different moral systems can provide for a heuristically useful way of seeing how different kinds of rights are generated and the various ways in which rights manifest themselves. Here, we wish to explore some of the basic ways in which these more theoretical issues can be used to ground a

Table 2.1. Types of Rights and Duties

Legal and political	Rights and corresponding duties are derived from a particular legal and political system and outline rules for minimal compliance
Relational (professional, organizational, personal)	Rights and corresponding duties derived from joining a professional body or organization or from other voluntary relationships (e.g., promising)
Moral	Rights and corresponding duties derived from a particular moral system (e.g., deontology, utilitarianism, libertarianism, etc.), which may or may not be reflected in, but provide a means for morally evaluating, legal, political, professional, or organizational ethics

basic understanding of rights that acknowledges what we take to be some basic features of rights and obligations that are generally defensible.

Perhaps the most straightforward justification for and explication of our moral rights and obligations is found in what is referred to as deontological or duty based ethics. Deontological theories take rights to form the basic moral units that undergird all of our social interaction. Such theories typically describe rights as necessary for protecting and fostering the inherent worth and dignity of human beings regardless of the contingent features that distinguish them. As a chief proponent of deontological ethics Immanuel Kant famously stated that one ought never to treat another person as a mere means to an end.[6] For Kant, persons possess the ability to engage in rational and autonomous thought and therefore possess inalienable and nontransferable rights. To treat a person as a mere means on this view is to treat a person as one would use an object, without regard for his or her rational capacity. So, for instance, in Kant's view lying to someone in order to get what we want is wrong precisely because it takes away the ability of the person lied to to rationally consent to the endeavor.

Importantly, Kant does not claim that we cannot use people as means to our own ends, since we must do so all of the time to achieve our ordinary ends. Instead, he claims that we cannot use them as mere means, without any regard for their status as rational persons. The difference really amounts to the difference between using someone as a mere thing for our own purposes versus engaging in interactions that are based in mutual consent and respect for the other. The rights of personhood stemming from our rational nature on this view necessarily entail the obligation of other rational beings to respect this fundamental feature of our personhood. Among the corresponding obligations required to properly respect another's right to be treated with dignity and respect are the categorical obligations to not deceive other persons or steal from them and the duty to continually try to develop and support rationality and autonomy.

While strict deontological theories accent the inherent moral worth of persons, other theories attempt to show that rights and duties are also often described as necessary for establishing and maintaining the integrity of our social practices. Philosophers and social theorists stressing the importance of social integrity note that without established and respected moral rights and duties, social practices tend to undercut trust, cooperation, and solidarity and promote deceptive, and often violent, behavior.[7] In a free market this would threaten the willingness of buyers, investors, and sellers to exchange capital and other things that they value. The benefits of a free market require recognizing and promoting certain proper moral rights and sentiments, such as respecting the right to private property, liberty, and nondeception. Without a respect for these more universal moral rights free exchange may give way to morally unscrupulous actions. Indeed, one major contributing factor in the most recent financial meltdown was the prevalence of fraud and deception. Among other things, this undercut the ability of investors to assess risk and consequently froze the flow of capital.

Identifying and respecting moral rights and duties is thus necessary for establishing and maintaining both individual integrity and that of our social practices. Given our analysis in the last chapter this should lead to measurable results in terms of driving company success, perhaps most explicitly in helping to develop and maximize social capital and trust. Even if in individual cases it does not, respecting certain moral rights, for example, human rights, ought to take precedence over other obligations to do what is good and what is right. However, even if we recognize the basic importance of rights, there is always the potential for different rights and obligations to conflict in practice. For instance, while often many stakeholder rights align with both each other and with other managerial obligations, inevitably conflict between various stakeholder rights and managerial obligations will occur. Different moral theories tend to offer different theoretical models for accounting for and resolving these conflicts of various rights and obligations. Here, while avoiding a lengthy analysis of the nature of these theoretical discussions, we will provide an overview of some of the ways in which talk of rights and duties can be further parsed in order to better understand and approach such potential conflicts. In our view, providing for such a more exacting rights-based terminology allows managers to better prioritize stakeholder rights and duties and respond to ethical dilemmas in the workplace.

Fundamental Rights and Duties

As most people recognize that some rights have a greater significance than others, we can make an initial distinction between different sorts of rights based upon the "weight" that they carry. In our model, what we recognize that "fundamental rights" refer to the rights that are the weightiest in nature. We take it that these rights are inherently valuable and that the duties that they give rise to ought to receive the highest priority and ought always to be respected. Following Thomas Donaldson, we will say that fundamental rights: (1) protect something that is vitally important, (2) are subject to significant and recurring threats, and (3) fairly distribute the economic distribution of the duties they impose.[8] Expanding upon the third criterion, we find that respecting fundamental rights, driving company success, and maximizing value are compatible. But, stated more forcefully, we regard the right to exist as a corporation contingent upon respecting fundamental rights. As such, if a company cannot be successful while at the same time respecting fundamental rights it is fair to impose economic burdens or other sanctions that may compromise the economic solvency of that company.

Expanding upon the first criterion we further define "vitally important" in two ways. Something is vitally important if (a) it is necessary for promoting and protecting individual integrity, dignity, and respect or (b) if it is regarded as necessary for a crucial social practice to exist or flourish. Human rights fall under the category of (1a). An abbreviated version of the UN Declaration on Human Rights is included in Appendix D.[9] Rights and duties that are necessary to promote and sustain value creation and accepted market conditions fall under (1b). These rights and duties tend to protect private property, liberty, ensure fair competition and shareholder trust, contracts, and deter fraud.

Derivative Rights and Duties

Derivative rights and duties are not logically or practically essential for individual integrity or the integrity of social practices and may be justifiably infringed upon, at times, if they conflict with other important rights or interests. Following noted business ethicists Joseph DesJardins and John McCall, derivative rights "depend for their importance on an instrumental contribution toward achieving some other good."[10] Even in such cases when infringing upon another's right is justifiable, this does not, however, deny the importance of these rights. So, the imposition of derivative rights must in some way balance and suitably protect the conflicting interests involved. Thus in order to protect competing interests and rights, infringing upon a derivative right requires significant *warrant*. While such rights might be occasionally waived, they are not to be routinely ignored.

Privacy is an illustrative example of a derivative right. Privacy rights are certainly very important and to a large degree necessary for the development of individual autonomy and for sustaining important relationships, such as those found in doctor–patient and lawyer–client relationships.[11] In our public and private lives, however, privacy can be justifiably infringed upon if there is good cause, given competing moral concerns. For instance, we might justifiably breach someone's privacy in order to protect national security or respond to the commission of a serious crime. However, even in doing so, we would require a formal degree of warrant in order to justify the breach of privacy. In such cases, we need to balance the interests in security or public welfare against those of privacy. In our view, violations of derivative rights are only justified if there is another significant moral imperative that can only be served by violating such a right and the violation in question is done in the least extensive manner possible.

In business, privacy rights are also regarded as important, both for individuals and for the protection of corporate interests. On one hand, businesses require information that may otherwise be considered private (e.g., employee criminal background, financial status, medical history or sensitive consumer information) in order to protect their interest. On the other hand, privacy rights may include certain freedoms deemed important both inside and outside of the work setting (e.g., freedom of expression, association, and autonomous identity formation). As in our lives out of work, in business privacy rights can likewise be infringed upon if there is good cause. For example, an employee's right to privacy can be infringed if the private information sought about the employee is relevant to their job performance or perhaps if there is no expectation of privacy or implied consent. In such cases employee privacy rights give way to the company's associative right to protect its interests. Infringing privacy and other derivative rights can, however, go too far. As the relationship between employee public and private life erodes, more fundamental rights directly related to human liberty, freedom, and association may begin to be violated. As such, the notion of warrant must be taken seriously and the two restrictions placed on justifiable violations of rights taken with the utmost seriousness. In particular, there is some debate regarding the use of the job relevance standard and the potential for corporate abuse.[12]

Negative and Positive Duties

As previously mentioned, where there is a right there is a corresponding obligation to respect that right and, as such, rights generate duties. It is important to note that we can respect rights in different ways. Some forms of respect require inaction while other forms of respect require action. With this in mind, we can also distinguish negative from positive rights and duties. Negative rights and duties require a person to *refrain* from performing some action and do not require additional support or aid. For example, I can discharge my obligation to respect another person's freedom of speech and expression by simply refraining from acts of censorship. I am not obliged to agree with the person or take additional steps or spend additional resources to protect their speech or come to their aid when their right to speak freely is violated. On the other hand, positive duties impose affirmative obligations to in some way support (e.g., provide resources) or come to the aid of another person whose rights are being violated. While I as an individual do not have a positive duty to protect and support another's entitlement to speak freely, others certainly do. In a constitutional democracy, for example, security forces are often required to provide support to ensure that the right to free speech is protected and to come to the aid of those whose right to free speech is violated.

For some time, rights and managerial obligations in business were viewed by many as being merely negative in nature. The argument was that managers needed only to attend to the positive responsibilities of shareholders and as long as they did not violate other person's rights to freely pursue their own interests, say by theft or fraud, they had discharged all of their obligations. As mentioned earlier, this amounts to a rather myopic view of managerial obligations. In the context of our discussion, relationships with stakeholders generate both negative and positive fundamental and derivative rights and duties.

With regard to fundamental rights, for example, Donaldson argues that certain international rights, which hold regardless of the country or region in which a company operates, generate some rather clear negative and positive obligations. While companies should never directly deprive community members of their property rights, they are not necessarily obliged to protect or aid community members from local governmental infringement. Alternatively, the right to nondiscriminatory treatment generates both negative and positive obligations. For example, a company ought never to discriminate on the basis of race or gender. Companies are further obligated to ensure that corporate cultures, policies, and procedures do not promote discriminatory conduct. Other positive responsibilities requiring additional time, resources, and managerial attention include the following: promoting a healthy, safe, and secure workplace, providing educational opportunities for underage workers, providing a wage that enables employee subsistence, and promoting supply-chain and industry wide efforts to improve the political and civil conditions of host countries. Donaldson's list of nonexhaustive fundamental rights and corresponding positive and negative obligations is featured in Table 2.2.[13]

As an example of positive obligations tied to a derivative right, an employer must refrain from infringing upon employee privacy rights

Table 2.2. Fundamental International Rights and Obligations

Fundamental right	Negative obligation to refrain from depriving	Positive obligation to protect
Freedom of physical movement	x	
Ownership of property	x	
Freedom from torture	x	
Fair trial	x	
Nondiscrimination	x	X
Physical security	x	X
Freedom of speech and association	x	X
Minimal education	x	X
Political participation	x	X
Subsistence	x	X

without good reason. This requires that some positive action (e.g., relating the private information sought to reliable performance metrics) must be taken to ensure job relevance. Additionally, if a human resource department holds sensitive, private employee or even consumer information, they are positively obligated to ensure that this information is reasonably protected from opportunistic exploitation. This might require procedural protocols and use of protective, security enhanced information technologies.

As mentioned in chapter 2, rights and positive obligations can also arise in certain situations when companies are in a position to promote a greater good or prevent harm. The obligation to engage in environmentally sustainable business is of this kind. Engaging in sustainable business development requires additional resources and if held to be a duty would certainly constitute a positive obligation. Authors point out that a failure to engage in sustainable business development will lead to grave ecological and ethical disasters as the biosphere's ability to sustain life is potentially threatened by such economic activity. Additionally, the harms inflicted will hurt those who are both least advantaged and those who are least likely to have contributed to large scale environmental degradation in the first place. Businesspersons are in a position to effectively engage in sustainable environmental practices without compromising, and in our account even improving, their competitive advantage. In fact, some companies are in a unique position to promote change. The case of Ford's influence on its supply chain is such an example. Accordingly, businesses that meet these criteria ought to engage in sustainable business development.[14] The argument is valid and so if these premises are true the following conclusion holds. And, we, perhaps as community stakeholders or even armchair activists, have the moral right to expect that businesses will move in this direction.[15] Failure to do so may not violate the law, but it would violate an important positive moral obligation and would require very good reasons to do so.

Special Obligations

Additionally, defining that which constitutes a special obligation provides another way to help identify other positive rights and duties.

Special obligations are relatively strong moral obligations and as such tend to take priority over other positive responsibilities that we may have. As the philosopher Robert Goodin explains, special obligations arise out of particular relationships in which there is a high degree of vulnerability and dependence. Conditions that contribute to a high degree of vulnerability and dependence are as follows. (1) There is an asymmetrical balance of power between the parties in the relationship. (2) One party needs the resources, products, or services provided by the relationship to protect very important or fundamental interests. (3) The party in need can only advance their interest vis-à-vis the relationship with the superordinate party. (4) The superordinate party exercises a high degree of discretionary control over resources and thus over the subordinate party's interests. These conditions can arise naturally or by social convention.[16]

When particularly acute conditions of vulnerability and dependence do arise they typically leave the subordinate or needier party open for opportunistic exploitation. Generally speaking, when persons are particularly vulnerable, there is a special obligation to protect them from opportunistic exploitation and to come to their aid when such exploitation exists. This obligation is typically grounded within the kind of relationship that exists between two parties. For instance, relationships that generate special obligations include those between parents and children, guardians and wards, doctors and their patients, and lawyers and their clients. Children, wards, patients, and legal clients are in a position where they need special attention and where they must trust that their benefactors are acting in their interests. Likewise, in entering into a relationship with these persons, such agents take on special obligations to promote and protect their wellbeing.

In business, certain managerial relationships with stakeholders evidence acute degrees of vulnerability and dependence. The manager–shareholder relationship is one of them. Alexei Marcoux describes the relationship as follows. The agential aspect of shareholder–manager relationships is limited-access as shareholders turn over limited control of their assets to a management team for a specific purpose. The management team possesses the day-to-day relevant knowledge about the health of the company, makes decisions about how to allocate resources, and controls the flow of information to shareholders. Shareholders are not aware of the day-to-day operations of a firm and must rely on intermittent, sophisticated, and at times, easily manipulated reports. Due in large part to this control and informational asymmetry, shareholder interests may be harmed by the opportunistic exploitation of their trust without them knowing it. This relationship tends to contrast with typical managerial relationships with other stakeholders (e.g., employees, suppliers, consumers, or communities, etc.), where harms are often known when they occur and whose relationship is readily severable as soon as harm occurs.[17] Managers thus have a special, fiduciary responsibility, grounded in a special moral obligation, to exercise a degree of honesty, care, and loyalty and all things being equal place company success ahead of other interests. In this sense, companies that cannot at a particular time design and implement a comprehensive and formal environmentally sustainable business plan and remain economically solvent or otherwise competitive ought not to do so. This would not mean, however, that they perhaps should not do anything. Obligations to enact less resource dependent efforts to be environmentally responsible would remain.

The fiduciary metaphor may be stretched too far if extended to other stakeholder relationships and lose legal clarity and force in doing so. Nevertheless, other particularly high degrees of vulnerability and dependence do exist between managers and stakeholders, and to such a degree as to warrant special obligations. Employees living in abject poverty clearly meet the conditions for acute vulnerability and dependence. These employees are often underage, malnourished, undereducated or even illiterate, and quite desperate for any form of employment. Choosing to work in unfavorable conditions does not eliminate this vulnerability and dependence nor does it absolve employers of their moral responsibilities. In fact, this vulnerability and dependence leads to such things as physical and psychological abuse, sexual exploitation, unacceptable risks and threats to employee health and safety, torturous working conditions, and sustained bondage. The continued existence of sweatshops attests to these realities.[18]

Managerial relationships with consumers also reflect high degrees of information vulnerability and dependence. Many products like derivative bundles and even some mortgages and insurance policies are terribly sophisticated and require expert advice. Salespersons purport to act in the interest of their customers and, even if not formally recognized as a fiduciary, are in a position to opportunistically exploit consumer trust. Even in areas where there is extensive legislative oversight, consumers are unlikely to know about the health risks related to pharmaceuticals unless the manufacturer discloses them. Thus manufacturers can be said to have a special obligation with regard to product safety issues, regardless of whether or not "safety sells." Likewise, underage consumers are typically highly vulnerable to marketing and advertising efforts and given the prevalence of ads may not be sufficiently protected by parental or other consumer advocacy groups. As such, child consumers tend to require a higher and more positive degree of managerial care and protection.

Stakeholder Rights and Obligations

As noted above, focusing too exclusively on shareholder rights and corresponding duties can narrowly focus managerial vision in a manner that impairs the ability to recognize other equally and at times more important legal, political, professional, and moral rights. Managing for integrity thus requires expanding managerial vision to consider a wider set of stakeholder rights. As mentioned previously, moving in this direction can be problematic, especially when stakeholder rights and corresponding obligations conflict. The rights-based terminology just developed will help managers work through moral conflict and prioritize claims. While we do not claim that the following steps for addressing stakeholder rights and duties will eliminate all controversy, they will certainly provide some moral clarity and a helpful framework for continued discourse. Such an approach provides sufficient means for addressing a wide range of issues and problems in a morally defensible manner and responding constructively to the most controversial issues. Further, implementing such an approach will help solidify organizational integrity in such a manner as to allow management to avoid further dilemmas in the future.

First, managers need to begin by identifying fundamental stakeholder rights and corresponding negative and positive duties in their strategic planning. It is very important to understand that stakeholders may have fundamental rights even if they fail to express them. An impoverished worker in a developing nation, for example, has inalienable and fundamental human rights even if he or she does not try to or are not in a position to leverage them.

Additionally, managers should also identify those relationships that exhibit acute degrees of vulnerability and dependence. These relationships will generate positive managerial actions to protect stakeholders from exploitation and, where necessary, come to their aid. Fundamental duties and special obligations should be identified as critical path points that must be met in order to morally justify maximizing company value and driving company success. Stated differently, value ought never to be maximized and company success achieved at the expense of violating fundamental rights, duties, and special obligations. This does not mean that the relative costs of respecting fundamental rights and duties should not be calculated. In fact, companies should and can respect these rights in very different but efficient ways. It does mean, however, that fundamental rights and special obligations ought to be seen as having an inherent degree of value and thus take priority over other rights and interests.

Second, managers should identify and prioritize derivative stakeholder claims and corresponding negative and positive rights and duties. Unlike fundamental rights and duties, when considering derivative rights and duties it is acceptable and appropriate to balance them off against other goods and claims. In particular, that which is good for company success and best promotes value can and ought to guide and shape these considerations. When overriding a derivative right, however, managers must take appropriate care to justify their decision. This justification must balance and do justice to the other goods and rights involved. For example, failing to implement a comprehensive environmental sustainability program would require justification. Where possible, alternatives that allow such rights to be preserved while pursuing corporate value must be pursued as well. Finally, managers should also be aware that the continued infringement of derivative rights and duties may not be justified and may begin to impact more fundamental rights. This was previously illustrated in the case of employee privacy rights. The same case can be made in terms of environmental sustainability programs. Continued failure to implement more comprehensive sustainability programs may end up violating the fundamental rights of persons in developing nations and/or threaten the earth's productive capability and thus threaten business as a social practice.[19] In addition to prioritizing fundamental rights and special obligations, certain derivative rights and duties ought to take priority over others. Bringing these considerations into stakeholder analysis is critical.

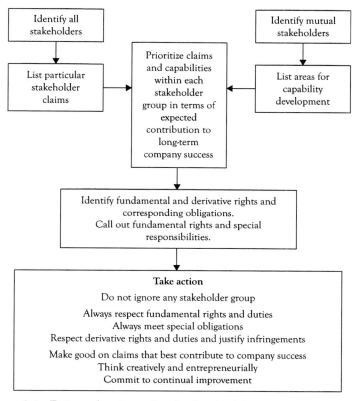

Figure 2.1. Doing what is good and what is right.

Once more, we do not deny that identifying and categorizing stakeholders and prioritizing corresponding fundamental, derivative, and corresponding negative, positive, and special obligations can be a difficult task. Indeed, an overly simplistic appraisal of stakeholder rights and managerial obligations may cause more harm than good. However, in the next chapter we provide a management system model that will help make this process of identification and analysis more straightforward. In the remainder of this chapter, we will describe some of the prominent stakeholder rights and corresponding duties. Again, this list is meant to be illustrative and not completely exhaustive. Likewise, though we believe that the list includes rights and duties that are widely accepted and generally defensible, we acknowledge that some disagreement may remain with regard to particular items.

Competitors

In general, competitors have a right to expect fair competition and managers have negative duties to refrain from actions that undercut fair competition. Specific rights and duties vary from region to region but tend to be legally defined in the areas of corporate, antitrust, and anticorruption laws and regulations. Most rules and regulations include duties to refrain from such things as price fixing, pricing lower than cost, or creating artificial barriers for market entry in order to force out smaller businesses, using bribery or kickbacks to promote competitive advantage, and respecting intellectual and other private property rights. As the notion of fair competition is fundamental for a market economy to exist and flourish, we regard these rights as fundamental to business practices. At a minimum, these rights and corresponding duties generate weighty obligations for legal compliance. Furthermore, joint arrangements or partnerships with competitors would create additional rights and obligations, particularly the duty to acquiesce to accepted rules of association.

Shareholders

Respecting shareholder rights can also be seen as morally fundamental as shareholder trust and informed risk assessment is regarded as practically necessary for capital investiture. As previously noted, managerial relationships with shareholders, particularly at the executive level of management, give rise to degrees of acute vulnerability and dependence. Thus managers have special and fundamental obligations to shareholders, which at least in part morally ground fiduciary and other legal obligations. As stated earlier, to discharge these obligations a manager must advance shareholder interests ahead of securing their own private interests, provide a fair return on investment, and exercise a degree of loyalty, care, and honesty that is above and beyond that found in typical market relationships. Managerial obligations to shareholders also include ensuring that others effectively and efficiently fulfill their nominal functions and terms of employment per defined job descriptions. Additionally, managers must operate with the utmost fiscal transparency and truthfully disclose all conflicts of interest and forms of compensation and ensure that others do the same. Furthermore, managers must honestly report on company financial performance and promote internal auditor compliance. Various fundamental and special obligations manifest in legal (e.g., English common law or equity law) and regulatory governance and accounting initiatives. These initiatives include the US Sarbanes–Oxley Act and the Principles of Corporate Governance offered by the Organization for Economic Cooperation and Development (OECD). Appendix E provides a list of shareholder rights referenced in the OECD principles and a summary of the accounting and financial reporting and disclosure requirements under theSarbanes–Oxley Act.[20]

Employees

Like competitors and shareholders many employee rights and managerial duties are codified in law. The extent to which employee rights and corresponding managerial duties are recognized and enforced varies from region to region and country to country. Regardless of national and international variations, however, the fundamental rights and positive and negative obligations listed in Table 2.2 apply to employees.[21] While these rights and duties may seem obvious for some, situations of acute vulnerability and dependence and instances of sweatshop labor down company supply chains continue to abound and should receive special attention. More specifically, to the extent that companies often have the knowledge that these abuses are occurring and are often in a position to effectively and efficiently influence supplier conduct, they (individually and/or as an industry) are morally responsible for improving working conditions sufficient to meet minimal, fundamental rights and duties.[22]

Managers also have the positive obligation to provide employees with meaningful work. For Kantians, meaningful work is work that allows an employee to exercise some degree of autonomy on the job and offers opportunities for personal development. Along Kantian lines, the obligation to provide meaningful work is viewed as an imperfect obligation, or obligation that can be fulfilled in a variety of different manners. In our account, the right meaningful work is a derivative right, but one that we ought to nonetheless always strive to actualize. Providing meaningful work represents a very important obligation, as there is a deep connection between work and individual dignity and self-respect. Following Kantian reasoning, one ought never to treat other persons as mere tools, cogs in a machine, or mere means to an end.

The Kantian business ethicist and management consultant Norman Bowie endorses the following characteristics of meaningful work.[23] First, meaningful work allows the employee to exercise autonomy on the job. The nature and extent of autonomous decision-making and employee participation will necessarily vary from job to job. Yet, even in aline working in a high volume production factory a manager can discharge this obligation by providing the employee with some degree of choice regarding the job that they are doing and how best to do it. In other more proactive cases managers employ open management styles and foster employee ownership and governance structures. Second, meaningful work helps to promote an employee's rational development. Managers can provide training opportunities that open up new job opportunities and encourage both lateral and upward mobility. Third, meaningful work does not hinder and even helps to promote employee moral development. Managers thus ought to strive to create a positive organizational ethical culture and not put employees in positions that make it difficult to do the right thing. Fourth, meaningful work provides a fair wage. Fifth, meaningful work is not paternalistic. A mark of paternalistic management is to think that you always know what's best, to micro-manage, and to fail to grant employees the independent responsibility and authority to make decisions. While some degree of paternalism may be necessary, a manager must remember that they are managing autonomous human beings and ought not to treat such persons as children. In addition to Bowie's principles we would add that meaningful work clearly relates the employee's work to a higher cause (e.g., long-term company success, environmental and social responsibility, etc.). Figure 2.2 illustrates these principles.

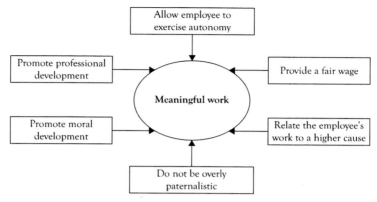

Figure 2.2. Principles of meaningful work.

A scholar and organizational consultant, Bowie highlights successful companies who have profitably embraced the notion of meaningful work. These companies include Miller Furniture, Hewlett-Packard, and IBM. More recently, Kimberly-Clark, a long-time world leader in consumer tissue products, was recently ranked number in the world's 25 best multinational companies to work for.[24] Their commitment to meaningful work is an explicit part of their mission and regarded as a key to their sustained success.

> At Kimberly-Clark, we thrive because our employees bring passion and commitment to their work, their teams, their company and their world. We provide the opportunity to grow through meaningful work and professional development. You will be charged with delivering results as part of a diverse team.
>
> Our culture encourages open dialogue and the sharing of ideas, and recognizes innovation is the path to personal growth and corporate success. We operate on a first-name basis with a focus on always thinking about our customer, building trust, and building our talent. We have a strong emphasis on making decisions, continuously improving our business and processes and a strong aim to win on a consistent basis.[25]

Employees have other moral rights that may be derivative and defensible (at least in the workplace) but are nevertheless very important as their continued infringement may undercut more fundamental rights and even severely impact the ability for value creation. As mentioned these rights include the right to privacy and the corresponding managerial obligation to ensure that infringements are relevant to job performance.

In other democratic nations citizens have the fundamental right to due process, while private employees, at least in the United States, do not have due process rights in the workplace and may be hired, fired, promoted, or demoted at will. Regardless of legal standing, arbitrarily evaluating employee potential or actual performance is morally unjustifiable. Along Kantian lines, some point out that the employment at will policy (or at least making decisions without justification or warrant) reduces a person to a mere thing or a mere piece of property. [26] Additionally, as hiring and firing harms an employee (e.g., in terms of loss of salary and ability to find new employment) it is prima facie wrong to do so without justification or warrant. Furthermore, instances where employees are fired, hired, promoted, or demoted on the basis of their attitudes toward political, ethical, and social issues are increasing.[27] This raises larger concerns about free speech and autonomy, may in fact be discriminatory and violate civil rights, and also seems to violate the managerial duty to shareholders to advance company interests over personal or private beliefs. So, while perhaps falling short of a formal due process system, managers have the positive obligation to ensure that decisions regarding hiring, firing, demotion, and promotion are justified and the reasons for such decisions be shared.

Consumers

Fundamental consumer rights and special managerial obligations tend to focus on product safety and truth in advertising. Regarding product safety, respective managers are obligated to exercise due care in product design, development, and production. This includes taking extra care to recognize, detect, and prevent defects that would adversely impact consumer health or create and unreasonably dangerous product. Managers also have the responsibility to take extra care when consumers are especially vulnerable and dependent on the manufacturer for safety information. On such occasions safety risks for nondefective products must be clearly and truthfully disclosed. Additionally, managers may be morally responsible, if not legally liable, for the misuse of nondefective products provided the managerial action knowingly contributes, anticipates, and benefits from product misuse. Contribution to misuse can occur in the product design, sales and marketing, and distribution stages. Tobacco companies, for example, that intentionally design addictive products, pitch these products to underage consumers, and lobby for weak regulation would meet the conditions for such failures of obligations. In such cases the notion of "social product liability" is said to apply.[28]

Related to health and safety issues deception in marketing, advertising, and sales is particularly egregious. However, even where product safety is not an issue, deception, or the intent to get a consumer to act upon a false belief can be argued to violate a fundamental right. In general the right to not be deceived and to be told the truth is regarded as derivative. Deception may be warranted where the deceptive act is necessary to prevent a greater harm, where deception is an accepted feature of the practice, say in the game of poker, or there is no harm caused, as in the case of a "white lie." In business, however, these conditions do not apply. Deception in sales and marketing does not prevent a great harm. While it may be prevalent in some industries, deception is not morally accepted as it is in poker. Additionally, consumers are regularly harmed by deceptive sales tactics and express their indignation and loss vis-à-vis lawsuits. It is important to recognize that deception circumvents consumer autonomy and their capacity for rational decision-making. Kantians regard such actions as categorically or fundamentally immoral regardless of the consequences. Consequentialists, such as Adam Smith, regard the rational pursuit of self-interest as fundamental for market efficiency and overall social welfare. On both justifications, deception in marketing, advertising, and sales is fundamentally wrong. And as in the case of product safety, the duty to take extra care to protect consumers who are especially vulnerable and dependent on deceptive sales tactics constitutes a special obligation. Managers thus have fundamental and often special obligations to refrain from deception or otherwise avoid advertising techniques that would end up deceiving a reasonable person.[29]

In addition to fundamental rights, managers have very important derivative obligations to consumers. The obligations to create a quality product and establish systems to promote product quality are prime examples of such obligations. As defined by the International Organization of

Standardization, product "quality" is broadly defined as a product that meets explicit and implicit customer expectations and extends beyond safety considerations. The widely utilized family of ISO 9000 and related standards establishes a framework for effectively and efficiently assuring product quality. Product safety and issues of deception aside, managers have the right to sacrifice product quality for other more immediate concerns and forgo the sometimes costly process of designing, implementing, and maintaining a quality management system. In some situations it may be practically impossible to give customers all that they want. Such cases, however, should be regarded as managerial failures or at least opportunities for improvement and actions should be taken to remedy or improve the situation. Continued failure to provide quality products will severely impact if not permanently destroy a company's ability to create value. Given the importance of value and supply chain management, positive managerial obligations may also extend to promote quality management system methods and practices in their supply chain.

Suppliers

Contractual obligations to suppliers can be regarded as fundamental, as respect for contractual agreements is central to business relations and typically legally protected. More controversial are duties to improve supply chain working conditions and positive work to eliminate sweatshops. Company and managerial obligations to do so may stem from the fundamental positive obligations to promote secure, healthy, and safe work conditions referenced earlier. Does this obligation extend down a company supply chain? We agree with those who argue that companies do in fact have a moral responsibility in this regard. Philosophers tend to identify two conditions that if met make agents morally responsible for their actions. First, the agent must have reasonable knowledge about the harms or benefits their actions will have. Second, the agent must have sufficient and reasonable power to take actions that can effectively improve the situation or help to mitigate harms. In terms of the first condition, any reasonable businessperson in the textile, agricultural, and various manufacturing sectors understands their supply chain well enough and is (or at least ought to be) aware of the realities of sweatshop labor. Additionally, while companies are certainly not the sole causes of the conditions that promote sweatshop labor, many are (whether individually or collectively) in the position to leverage their power to improve supply chain conditions. Some define this responsibility as a moral right and fundamental obligation.[30] Others could describe this moral responsibility as a positive and special obligation that stems from the company–supplier relationship and the acute vulnerability of sweatshop workers. In any event, the obligation to improve working conditions in companies, down supply chains, and across industries is morally paramount.

Government

Governments and their agencies and the communities of citizens they represent are also stakeholders of corporate activities, due to the manner in which corporate activities might intersect with governmental activity. For instance, pharmaceutical companies often interact with governmental health agencies, and the manner in which they cooperate with those agencies can significantly affect the ability of those agencies to effectively carry out their publicly charted goals. Minimally, governmental stakeholders and citizens have a right to expect legal compliance and companies have a duty to comply.

Communities

The relationship between companies, governments, and communities, however, often creates moral obligations beyond legal compliance. While the relationships that businesses have with the communities in which they operate often lack the status to ground fundamental rights, in our view they nonetheless give rise to important derivative rights and, at times, can even ground certain other fundamental rights. Certainly, at a minimum, businesses have a fundamental negative duty not to violate certain basic rights of community members. For instance, if environmental damage poses significant physical harms to the community in which a plant operates, then management has an obligation to end or mitigate such harms on the basis of the bodily rights of innocent members of that community not to be subjected to physical harm without their consent. Likewise, if not legal, moral restrictions on the types of environmental harms that companies can impose upon the communities in which they operate can be justified on the basis of fundamental property rights. Thus, in our view, managers need to consider the environmental impacts of their company activities not just because of the general, though derivative, obligation to promote greater value in society, but also because of the specific and fundamental obligation not to violate the negative rights of others. While we would hope that managers typically can find ways to contribute to the development of a greener economy more positively, at a minimum they ought not to engage in environmentally derogatory practices that substantially harm other community members.

Since many companies also operate in developing countries that lack many of the significant public safeguards that communities in Western countries provide for their citizens, companies have particular obligations toward members of these communities. In particular, Western managers should not ignore the significant potential for further destabilizing local communities if they do not carry out their operations with a mind toward community development. Of course, often companies can, and should, act as a catalyst to improve such communities as well, but at a minimum they should adopt the principle of "making no worse." The idea behind this principle is that due to the particularly vulnerable nature of communities in the developing world, companies have an obligation, at a minimum, not to make communities worse off than they would have otherwise been (had the company not engaged within the community). International development poses particular issues, and management should engage in relations with local communities on the principle that their relations should be mutually beneficial.

Other significant, though derivative, obligations that managers have toward the community stem from the special nature of the relationship that communities often establish with businesses. For instance, many communities provide tax breaks and other incentive packages in order to encourage businesses to locate or remain in their area. Companies that benefit from such arrangements incur a particular obligation, where possible, to act in ways that further benefit the community in which they operate. Aside from direct incentives, businesses benefit from their relationship to the community in other ways as well. For instance, communities help companies attract and retain desirable employees, provide necessary social services for employees, and work with companies to provide for the efficient planning of infrastructure and other public projects. In many ways, companies operate in reciprocal relationships with their communities, and as such they take on a special duty to provide for the good of the community, while still meeting their other basic obligations, where possible.

Other Stakeholder Issues

While the main kinds of company stakeholders are examined above, other stakeholders can also give rise to corporate obligations. For instance, ethnic or cultural groups may become stakeholders in virtue of the impact corporative activities may have on their social status. The debate over the use of Native American images in professional sports is a good example of such issues, and aptly raises the issue of how seemingly benign activities have the potential to determinately affect the social image of certain groups. The debate over advertising's effect on women is another example.[31] Many other ethical issues expressed by stakeholders raise other, larger issues regarding social justice, such as the fairness of executive compensation and the rich–poor gap.

Our purpose is not to give an exhaustive list of all possible stakeholders here, but to point out that indirect stakeholders may come in various forms, and managers have an obligation to be aware of these stakeholders and appropriately respond to any obligations toward such stakeholders that arise out of their activities. A basic principle of stakeholder analysis is that any person or group who can be affected by corporate activity is a potential stakeholder. This does not entail, in the view we are outlining here, that businesses are automatically obligated to put all stakeholders on the same level. What it does mean is that they should be aware of who such potential stakeholders are, how their activities might or might not impact them, what range of options—given their primary business aims—are available, and how they might maximize overall stakeholder value in light of such strategic considerations. Determining what sorts of rights and obligations might apply to these various groups, and how to balance and prioritize them is an essential part of this process.

Table 2.3 reflects that previous analysis, but describes various prominent stakeholder rights and corresponding obligation in a less technical manner.

Table 2.3. Summary of Prominent Stakeholder Rights and Managerial Obligations

Stakeholder	Rights and duties
Competitors	Right to expect fair competition (governments and citizens share this right) Always abide by antitrust, anticorruption, and other corporate laws. Companies should have a formal ethics and legal compliance system
Shareholders	Right to a fair return on investment Always make good on fiduciary responsibilities to act with the utmost loyalty, care, and honesty. Put company success ahead of conflicting interests (except where other fundamental rights are violated). Truthfully disclose financial performance. Take no material gain without consent. Ensure that compensation is valued relative to performance. Meet all regulatory requirements. Try to promote more positive and representative governance structures
Employees	Fundamental rights (see Table 2.2), right to meaningful work, right to privacy Never deprive employees of fundamental rights and protect fundamental rights where warranted, try to promote meaningful work, ensure that the private information sought is relevant to job performance, ensure that decisions regarding hiring, firing, promotion, and demotion are related to job performance (duties to shareholders require the same)
Consumers	Right to reasonable safe, nondefective products, right to know about product safety, right to expect truth in advertising Always exercise due care in design, production, and packaging, disclose all safety risks, never intend to deceive the customer, take special care with especially vulnerable and dependent consumers (e.g., children or consumers of very sophisticated and complex products), strive to implement a formal quality management system
Government and citizens	Right to legal compliance Always follow the law
Suppliers	Right to expect that contractual terms will be respected, employees have fundamental rights (see Table 2.2) Always respect contractual terms, negotiate and re-negotiate fairly, promote healthy and safe working conditions down the supply chain
Communities	Fundamental rights (see Table 2.2), right to healthy and safe environments Never violate fundamental rights, do not make communities worse off than they previously would have been, pay reparations or offer protection and aid when the company or its partners or associates violates fundamental rights, try to best engage in corporate social responsibility initiatives

Conclusion

Chapters 1 and 2 put us in a better position to understand what we ought to be doing as businesspersons and address the first two challenges identified in the book's introduction. Chapter 1 specifies the ends that we ought to seek in order to fully do what is good. Chapter 2 reminds us that in the pursuit of company success and overall social welfare we are not simply dealing with abstract stakeholder categories, but are dealing with persons and persons have specific rights that we are obligated to respect. Recognizing the basic principles associated with doing what is good and doing what is the right thing represent important achievements and will certainly help to promote ethical–organizational integrity. Nevertheless, this knowledge is worthless if one cannot bring these principles to bear in practice. Accordingly, chapter 3 outlines the features of effective ethics programs that help to establish and maintain an ethical–organizational culture.

Questions for Further Inquiry

Should companies violate the law when it is in their financial interest?

Are current forms of executive compensation fair?

Can companies be held legally liable for human rights violations down their supply chain?

Should sweatshop employees be paid higher than market conditions demands?

What are some of the best practices with regard to fighting human rights violations?

Are employee privacy rights being unduly infringed upon?

Is employment at will a fair and morally acceptable standard of employment?

Is it fair to hold a company liable for the social ills associated with product misuse?

CHAPTER 3

Ethics Programs

In the introduction to this book we identified three general challenges to promoting ethical–organizational integrity. The first was that while we may know that we ought to behave ethically and promote ethical conduct there often can be a lack of complete practical or philosophical consensus regarding what is good and right. The first two chapters address this challenge. Managers do that which is good by driving company success vis-à-vis understanding and meeting stakeholder claims, developing and leveraging mutual stakeholder capabilities, and in turn promoting long-term company success and social welfare. We also learned that in pursuing company success there are some things businesspersons ought never to do and, likewise, that they ought always to do. Our discussion of fundamental rights and special obligations helped to identify such duties. Furthermore, we relied on the distinction between derivative rights and positive obligations to help identify rights and duties that, all things being equal, managers ought to make good on, but could be justifiably waived in light of stronger competing obligations.

Despite the work done in chapters 1 and 2, there is a third challenge that stems more from considerations of the nature of decision-making and moral psychology than from the nature of moral claims themselves. The issue here has to do with developing moral character and motivating ethical conduct. For instance, even if managers possess strong theoretical framework for ethics, they will inevitably have to make decisions where the best thing to do and the right thing to do may not be entirely clear given the constraints of practical decision-making with limited time, information, and resources. Alternatively, managers may know very well what is good and right for their organization, but lack the organizational support or disposition to do it. This chapter will address these challenges. We begin by drawing on the ancient Greek philosopher Aristotle for some insight. We suggest that the goal of ethics programs should be to provide a practical framework to implement ethical-organizational integrity that allows individuals to overcome the practical barriers that often impede persons from coming to, and acting upon, ethical decisions. We then present the central features of effective ethics programs. Structuring ethics programs with these features in mind will help to effectively and meaningfully bring ethics and integrity to bear in practice.

Becoming Ethical

Knowing what ethics requires and becoming an ethical obligations person are challenging even though they are the two essential elements of a life worth living. The former requires considerable intellectual effort, while the latter requires building the right sort of character traits. Aristotle was one of the first philosophers to talk about the relationship between knowledge, character, and ethics and much of what he said still rings true today. Aristotle begins his Nicomachean Ethics with the simple observation that people desire or aim at that which they perceive as good.[1]

For most human beings, these goods include having friends and family, working and acquiring money, being proud of what we have accomplished and having a sense of self-worth, being entertained, humored, and experiencing pleasure, and being on the side of that which is just and right. While each of these goods individually contributes to a meaningful life, Aristotle points out that a person who truly flourishes will in one way or another have all of these elements in their lives and, as such, will live their lives to their fullest potential.[2] The good, as compared to individual goods, is a composite in this view, which includes the various goods that we aim at as parts of the good life.

Having it all in this sense, however, requires a great deal of balancing among competing goods. Consider the following examples. Working and earning money is good and is certainly necessary for us to accomplish many things in life. Work provides us with a meaning or purpose, and even a sense of identity. Money enables us to care for the persons we love and pursue our own life plans. However, excessively focusing on work and money may inhibit our ability to maintain meaningful relationships with family and friends. In some cases the pursuit of money turns into a greed that admits of no satisfaction. In such cases, money becomes seen as the highest good in its own right, and persons pursue it as if it alone could lead to satisfaction. Such a pursuit is disappointing at best, tragic at worst.

Experiencing bodily pleasure is good as well. We should have time for satisfying our more sensual desires and doing so leads to a degree of satisfaction. However, having a wanton personality and lacking self-control or moderation may lead one down the path of addiction. Again, such pursuit may lead to a tragic disregard for other goods that ends up depriving one of more lasting fulfillment in life. Having a positive sense of self-worth is also good and we should seek to distinguish ourselves from others and become great persons. Lacking a sense of humility and an ability to recognize and learn from one's mistakes, however, may lead to dangerous pride, as illustrated by the story of Icarus in Greek Mythology. Additionally, fear is a common human experience and when faced courageously helps us to prudently identify risks and avoid unnecessary harm. However, excessive fear may lead to cowardice and the lack of an appropriate amount of fear may lead us to make foolhardy decisions.

So in general, excessive or deficient dispositions or character traits, such as greed, gluttony, wantonness, recklessness, cowardice, vanity, insensibility, and irascibility, cause us to lose our balance and undermine our ability to truly flourish as human beings. Aristotle identifies excessive or deficient character traits or dispositions as vices.[3] In this sense, a vice is not just a moral failing, though it might well be that too, but it is also a simple failure of excellence. One who indulges in vice has failed to achieve the proper balance and inculcate the proper dispositions that would lead to a truly good life.

On the other hand, Aristotle describes composed and balanced character traits or dispositions as virtues. In other words, virtues are the means between dispositional extremes.[4] For Aristotle, being virtuous is the key to human flourishing because being virtuous best enables us to rationally assess situations, react appropriately, learn from our mistakes, and develop the character necessary to achieve a balanced life. This does not mean, however, that virtuous persons are always moderate, as the virtue of moderation relates specifically to experiencing pleasure. Consider the example of a general deciding whether or not to go into battle. A good general experiences some degree of fear or concern, perhaps about his life or the lives of his soldiers. A good general knows the right time to engage the enemy and the right time to retreat and is disposed to courageously act on that which is right without internal conflict. A bad general, however, who is engulfed by fear, might fail to properly engage the enemy causing potential harm to the larger cause and, as such, failing to benefit either himself or those who rely upon him. Behaving irrationally, a bad general may recklessly move his troops into battle or simply flee at the first sight of danger.[5]

To use one more example from Aristotle, we know that money is a good that most of us seek, but Aristotle argues that a virtuous person should here too follow a mean. While we should seek money to advance our own interests, the person of virtue should be liberal or generous with their money to others, since the good life is one of community. This does not mean, however, that a virtuous person gives their money to just anyone or that everyone needs to give in equal proportions. A virtuous person knows which causes are noble and promotes those kinds of causes. A virtuous person thus gives to the right people, at the right time, and in the right amount.[6] Accordingly, a virtuous person does not seek the mean or middle path relative to discrete actions, but cultivates dispositions that enable them to reason, act well, and ultimately live a full and meaningful life. The mean is relative to our dispositional characteristics and attitudes and not necessarily to particular acts. While we cannot escape our emotional reactions, we ought not to allow our emotions to cloud our moral vision or erratically direct our will. Indeed, our emotional responses must be cultivated to serve noble, virtuous, and ethical ends.

Knowing the right thing to do at the right time and in the right proportion and actually carrying it out does not always come naturally though. For Aristotle good judgment and action well requires a commitment to two things. First, we must be committed to learning and developing our cognitive capabilities as well as what Aristotle refers to as our intellectual virtues.[7] A good general, for example, studies a great deal of military history, strategy, and leadership theory. This fits very well with out discussion of capability developmental in chapter 1. Developing intellectual capacities and respecting intellectual virtues is, of course, not enough. Knowledge itself does not ensure good judgment. Nor does theoretical knowledge exhaust all possible situations a person might face and contexts in which he or she might act. Intellectual rules and principles can provide general guidelines, but no set of rules or principles can cover the particular features of all situations. In this sense, there is no single equation or set of theoretical rules that will tell us what we ought to do in any given situation in advance. Likewise, the practical nature of activity demands a stance that is not merely theoretical. One cannot, for instance, learn to ride a bike simply by knowing all of the mechanics of bicycles or aerodynamics. One must, simply put, learn to some extent by riding.

As such, Aristotle refers to the second component necessary for reasoning and acting well as a commitment to moral virtue.[8] A commitment to moral virtue requires habitual action (i.e., the sort of habitual action involved in practicing to ride a bike). In addition to learning about war, for example, becoming a good general demands practice in the field, so to speak. Generals and other soldiers are accordingly trained to act courageously and prudently in both simulated and actual battlefield experience. In this sense, courage cannot be learned in the classroom and learning about leadership does not in itself produce a good leader. During their training soldiers will inevitably make mistakes and less than optimal decisions, but over time and in the right conditions they will improve and develop intellectual and practical wisdom. Culture, organizational practices, and other environmental conditions obviously play a major role in either promoting or inhibiting virtuous behavior. Good militaries provide processes and an organizational culture that support intellectual and moral improvement and lead soldiers to act with integrity.

As with the development of effective generals, becoming a good and ethical businessperson requires the same sort of development. Making ethical decisions is not easy. In chapters 1 and 2 we provided some tools to help identify and prioritize that which is good and that which is right. A good businessperson knows the good and right thing to do in a situation and has the will to do it. Simply recognizing those actions we should never do (e.g., exploit children) and those that we always should do (e.g., promote company success) is not enough, as there will be situations where businesspersons do not know what ethics requires. How exactly should we structure our supply chain to eliminate exploitative labor practices? Given a variety of options how do we best manage stakeholders and drive and measure company success? How do we best accomplish such tasks given limited resources? All of the intellectual knowledge related to strategic management will not provide conclusive answers to these questions. Neither will theoretical knowledge promote the sort of virtuous dispositions that will prompt a person to act on what they may know is good and right. Unfortunately, many businesspersons know what is ethical and continually fail to act accordingly.[9] Ethical businesspersons, like good soldiers, require knowledge, practical experience, and the right sort of character traits. Additionally, good companies establish processes and an organizational culture that support intellectual and moral improvement and lead their stakeholders to act with integrity.

It is also important to note that as virtuous behavior is composite, the virtues and vices overlap. Additionally, and as Aristotle notes, it is often difficult to precisely define certain virtues. Although not exhaustive, Table 3.1 lists characteristic virtues and corresponding vices and provides a framework for character development.

BB&T Corporation, a U.S.-based financial holding company, is one firm that makes explicit reference to Greek philosophy and virtue. BB&T starts their value statement with the following preamble and list of important Aristotelian inspired virtues.

> The great Greek philosophers saw values as guides to excellence in thinking and action. In this context, values are standards which we strive to achieve. Values are practical habits that enable us as individuals to live, be successful and achieve happiness. For BB&T, our values enable us to achieve our mission and corporate purpose.
>
> To be useful, values must be consciously held and be consistent (non-contradictory). Many people have conflicting values which prevent them from acting with clarity and self-confidence.
>
> There are 10 primary values at BB&T. These values are consistent with one another and are integrated. To fully act on one of these values, you must also act consistently with the other values. Our focus on values grows from our belief that ideas matter and that an individual's character is of critical significance. Values are important at BB&T.

1. Reality (or fact based decision-making).
2. Reason (objectivity).
3. Independent thinking.
4. Productivity.

Table 3.1. *Virtues and Vices*

Excess	Virtue	Deficiency
Recklessness, a disposition to act without thinking, being out of control and acting irresponsibly	Courage and prudence in the face of danger or harm, ability to accurately assess risk and threats and take responsibility	Cowardice, fleeing in the face of danger, showing weakness when strength is required
Gluttony, hedonism, a disposition to overindulge	Moderation regarding bodily pleasures	Abstinence or asceticism
Self-effacing behavior, not taking care of one's own particular needs, crippling sorrow about the state of the world	Being concerned about the wellbeing of others and expressing empathy	Cold, egoistic, and insensitive dispositions, being hardhearted, cruel, or careless
Prodigality or being too loose with one's money, thinking that money will solve all problems	Being generous or liberal with one's personal wealth	Miserly, stingy, or greedy dispositions, being susceptible to corruption
Irascible or irritable and short-tempered behavior, being short-tempered	Being temperate with regard to one's emotional reactions, expressing righteous or noble indignation	Apathetic, unconcerned, or blasé dispositions
Being vain, vulgar, or narcissistic, showing conceit or arrogance	Striving for greatness in one's self and for others, having noble ambitions and a strong sense of self-worth	Being unambitious, being petty or too humble, thinking of one's self as irrelevant or inconsequential
Being a workaholic	Working hard at one's profession and being industrious	Being lazy, slothful, and always looking for the short-cut
Being too pedantic or snobbish, or being too candid, outspoken, and inappropriate	Seeking, knowing, and speaking the truth, being inquisitive	Dishonest, sophistical, cynical, or anti-intellectual behavior
Obsequious or sycophantic behavior, being overly superficial or too concerned about fitting in	Friendly, hospitable, and social dispositions, able to cultivate meaningful relationships that contribute to mutual flourishing	Cantankerous, disagreeable, unfriendly, or uninviting, being a loner
Losing touch with reality, living in a fantasy world, getting lost in possibilities	Being creative and imaginative, being a visionary	Dull, derivative, and insipid conduct, being unable to see things other than the way they appear

5. Honesty.
6. Integrity.
7. Justice.
8. Pride.
9. Self-esteem.
10. Teamwork.[10]

Given this analysis we can say that ethical-organizational integrity must include a commitment to developing intellectual and moral virtues. Persons with integrity desire to seek out that which is good and right and act accordingly. Organizations that promote ethical integrity will provide the structure and training in which such personal integrity can be inculcated. Building character and promoting virtue, however, is quite difficult. It is often difficult to find the right disposition and determine the right course to follow. People tend to be too prone to seeking immediate satisfaction and lack the vision and discipline to improve their situation. And, our institutions and cultures often tend to promote vices and ridicule virtues. In the next section, we lay out some of the principles behind, and characteristic features of, ethics programs that will help put your company on the right track.

Ethics Programs and Ethical–Organizational Integrity

As with many others in the field, we think that ethics programs should be structured to take a systematic and process oriented approach to building ethical–organizational integrity.[11] This involves designing processes for continual moral and intellectual development. While recognizing that ethical obligations are distinct from compliance or merely legal obligations, we nonetheless believe that compliance programs have much to offer structurally for those seeking to implement ethical programs for organizational integrity. For one, such programs are already present and widely understood within the business community. Second, they also tend to focus on how the organization, as a whole, integrates developmental issues.

As such, we suggest adopting the general model for promoting integrity that is suggested in the United States Federal Sentencing Guidelines and in quality management system standards. The US Federal Sentencing

Guidelines were first enacted in 1991 in order to introduce consistency into the federal sentencing process and increase the costs for corporations who engage in "white collar" crimes. Of particular interest for the field of business and organizational ethics, chapter 8 suggests a framework for structuring and assessing compliance programs and lays out basic organizational requirements for promoting good corporate citizenship. As opposed to focusing solely on individual culpability, the U.S. Sentencing Commission recognized that an organization is vicariously liable for the actions of its employees and may be indicted and subsequently fined if a federal crime is committed by those acting on its behalf. Organizations that failed to establish an effective compliance program could face penalties that increase base fines by up to a factor of four, raising the maximum possible fine for such corporations to $290,000,000. This "carrot and stick" approach to corporate sentencing was thus designed to both encourage proactive, well-structured, and robust compliance programs and severely punish organizational negligence. In order to mitigate fines and reduce pecuniary risk, an organization must exercise due diligence in a systematic effort to detect and eliminate criminal conduct.

The impact of the Federal Sentencing Guidelines of 1991 on corporate compliance programs has yielded mixed reviews. Some have argued that the Guidelines provide a compelling, flexible, and useful model for introducing and reinforcing legal and ethical conduct.[12] Even stronger claims suggest that the Guidelines' 7-step program serves as a model for standardizing international programs and proving a theoretical and practical foundation for teaching and training curriculum.[13] Others, however, point out that the 1991 Guidelines unduly conflate legality and ethics, as many legal compliance based programs do. The upshot of this argument is that good corporate citizenship is anemically reduced to following, or at least appearing to follow, the letter of the law and thus offers little incentive to promote well-grounded and substantive organizational change.[14]

Accordingly, the U.S. Federal Sentencing Guidelines were since revised. As commentators recognize, the new recommendations extend beyond mere legal compliance and suggest developing a more inclusive and robust notion of ethical–organizational integrity, as previously alluded to. In particular, suggestions distinguish legality from ethics and recommend that in addition to compliance managers should establish processes to engender an overall ethical organizational culture. Pursuant to this objective, the expectation is that effective ethics and compliance programs will at least supplement the punitive deterrence of criminal conduct with efforts to define and integrate core values and ethical commitments into organizational processes and positively inspire employees to "live up to the company's ethical ideals."[15]

The marked improvements over the 1991 guidelines are significant. First and foremost, the 2004 Guidelines now draw a strong connection between well-defined, shared, and culturally embedded organizational values and ethical commitments and lawful conduct. Furthermore, the revised Guidelines do not just rely on the standard, compliance based notions of rule definition, dissemination, detection, and punishment. In a much more positive sense, the revised Guidelines recommend incentivizing ethical behavior, encouraging active executive leadership and support, and ethics and compliance training. Finally, on a point often overlooked or otherwise underemphasized, the Guidelines now suggest that large organizations "should encourage small organizations (especially those that have, or seek to have, a business relationship with the large organization) to implement effective compliance and ethics programs."[16] As such, there is a movement to encourage ethical–organizational integrity down the supply chain and in effect across national and cultural boundaries. As many ethical and legal issues require global action beyond the doors of locally situated companies (e.g., issues concerning sweatshop labor and environmental degradation, pollution, and sustainability), this recommendation should not be underestimated. In light of marked improvements, the Guidelines' suggestions for structuring an ethics and compliance program and engendering intra- and interorganizational integrity bring a renewed sense of optimism. The Federal Sentencing Guidelines' newly revised chapter 8 suggestions are included in Appendix F.

Despite being developed by the U.S. judiciary the Federal Sentencing Guidelines provide succinct suggestions that are embraced by ethical–organizational integrity initiatives across the globe. They include the previously mentioned Ethical Compliance System 2000 and suggestions made in the OECD Guidelines for Multinational Organizations. For these reasons we find the U.S. Guidelines to have international appeal.

Our approach is also influenced by the International Organization for Standardization's quality oriented approach to management systems.[17]

This approach relies on certain basic principles. First, that leadership creates an environment where stakeholders are involved in organizational change and provides a clear and inclusive vision of the company's future. Second, goals are best achieved when persons and resources are managed within clearly established organizational processes. Third, that processes are regarded as pieces of an overall and clearly defined management system. Fourth, there is a firm commitment to measurable continual improvement at the individual, process, and management system level. Fifth, that process and the management system are periodically subject to the plan-do-measure-improve cycle. Managing for ethical–organizational integrity thus requires: (1) inclusive planning, setting, and documenting clear expectations and objectives, (2) responsible, accountable, process and systems oriented actions, (3) measurement and assessment, where unethical and illegal conduct are ultimately viewed as process failures, and (4) a firm and systematic commitment to becoming ethical.

The following provides somewhat standardized and flexible suggestions for designing, implementing, and maintaining an effective ethics program with the U.S. Federal Sentencing Guidelines and other similar global efforts, and quality management system principles in mind.

Features of Effective Ethics Programs

Documentation

Documentation plays a very important descriptive and normative role when managing for ethical–organizational integrity. In other words, ethics program documentation spells out, at all organizational levels, the descriptively relevant information for employees as well as the normative principles intended to guide the ethical framework of the organization. Regardless of the level of specificity, ethics program documentation should be subject to periodic review, should be understood by all employees, and should be objectively demonstrated in practice. It is also helpful to solicit appropriate stakeholder input when documenting ethical expectations, requirements, and goals. This requires different types and levels of documentation with varying degrees of specificity.

At the most general level, a company ought to document an *ethics vision statement*. An ethics vision statement should describe the higher normative ideals and standards to which all employees ought to aspire. The BB&T value statement offers such a vision. Additionally, the Johnson & Johnson credo, Novartis statement on human rights, and the Texas Instruments ethics and values statement provide similar and helpful states and are referenced in Appendix G. In general, well-written vision statements will:

- Include a clearly defined executive commitment to long-term company financial success and ethical and legal conduct. This commitment should stress that ethical and legal conduct and long-term company financial success are mutually dependent.
- Stress the importance of company stakeholders. The ethics vision statement should include overarching goals, such as commitments to product quality and safety, truth in advertising, environmental responsibility and sustainability, recognizing human rights, equal treatment and nondiscrimination, treating stakeholders with respect, promoting meaningful work and capability development, developing supply chains, ensuring legal compliance and fair competition, respecting privacy rights, and engaging in transparent and truthful financial reporting.
- Describe character traits that should be evidenced by stakeholders, which should include such virtues as honesty, courage, industriousness, prudence, loyalty, pride in one's work, justice, imagination, creativity and the ability to envision new possibilities, as well as a commitment to individual and organizational excellence.
- Include an executive commitment to establishing and maintaining an ethics program that is geared toward promoting, sustaining, and continually improving the company's ethical–organizational culture. There should also be a commitment to promoting ethical conduct and formalizing ethics programs within one's industry and across one's supply chain. As mentioned, the Federal Sentencing Guidelines stress the importance of larger companies taking the lead on this sort of initiative, particularly with regard to supply chain development.

- Provide a framework and an executive mandate for developing more specific and measurable objectives. As mentioned in the next section, each organizational process should have specific and measurable objectives related to promoting ethical conduct and preventing unethical conduct.
- Reference other appropriate ethics program documents, including ethics based regulations, ethical codes of conduct, and other supporting documents.

In addition to an ethics vision statement, management ought to document more specific *ethical codes of conduct*. Codes of conduct are more precise than an ethics vision statement and thus ought to spell out more concrete obligations. Well-written codes will:

- Reiterate the executive commitment to promoting ethical–organizational integrity and distinguish ethics from mere legal compliance. Employees should be aware that ethical codes of conduct do not exhaust ethics based requirements and will not cover all possible ethical issues, but that they do provide an overview of some of the most basic and important ethical requirements and commitments of the organization.
- Very clearly and concisely spell out specific duties and obligations and highlight fundamental rights, special obligations, and legal compliance duties. Codes of ethical conduct will thus focus more on defining and explaining the categorical or absolute ethical obligations necessary for minimal ethical compliance, as well as the ethical goals and values that should guide future development of organizational integrity.
- Specifically relate to particular job functions and organizational processes. There should be ethical codes for all organizational processes, including sales and marketing, finance and auditing, production, information technology, purchasing and supply chain management, human resources, and research and development, or engineering, as appropriate. Where appropriate, reference should be made to the standard ethics codes of particular relevant professional groups

(see Appendix C for the International Code of Ethics for Sales and Marketing as an example).

- Use examples to illustrate how to resolve common and recurring ethical issues.
- Be as specific as possible when explaining the repercussions for noncompliance, including but not limited to such things as employee dismissal or devaluing supplier performance. Again, these repercussions should be clearly spelled out relative to specific processes.
- Direct employees to ethics hotlines, the ethics officer, or other means for support if they should encounter an ethical dilemma or an ethical issue that extends beyond the scope of the code of conduct. Ethical codes should clearly explain when and under what conditions whistle blowing is permitted and not permitted.
- Reference other appropriate ethics-based documentation, including the ethics vision statement and other appropriate procedures, policies, and work instructions.

Finally, ethical expectations should be appropriately documented in organizational procedures, work instructions, forms, and other everyday documentation. Like ethical codes of conduct, working documents should include ethical requirements for each organizational process. For example, procedures and associated work instructions regarding how to close a sale should include rules about disclosure and nondeception. Additionally, forms could be developed to ensure that customers are aware of their rights. This, for example, is often accomplished in mortgage sales and lending with truth and lending disclosures and in providing as well as signing-off on a borrower's bill of rights. As another example, procedures and instructions for selecting and evaluating suppliers should rule out the use of sweatshop labor, along with appropriate definitions and resources for documenting what constitutes sweatshop conditions. Accompanying forms and records should demonstrate that such rules are being obeyed. Additionally, procedures regarding information technology should convey the moral importance of respecting and protecting customer and employee privacy rights and include specific protocols for securing sensitive data. This ensures continuity between the ethics vision statement, codes of ethical conduct, and everyday procedural activities.

Organizational Processes

One of the goals of an ethics program is to integrate ethics into everyday operations. Documenting ethical requirements in a company's ethics vision statement, codes of ethical conduct, and everyday procedures, work instructions, and forms contributes to this end. Other actions on organizational processes should include the following.

- Management should periodically document the flow of all organizational processes and identify the stakeholder interactions, expectations, and rights within these processes. The ethics vision statement, codes of conduct, and everyday documentation should be used to determine ethical expectations concerning employee and other relevant stakeholder behavior.
- Management should periodically conduct gap analyses to identify inconsistencies between documented expectations and the way things actually stand. For example, an ethics vision statement might claim to promote environmental responsibility and sustainability but organizational processes may not reflect this commitment. This would indicate a gap between normative expectations and empirical conduct. Management should then take steps to correct the situation. We will address the issue of corrective action in more detail when we discuss continual improvement.
- Management should periodically examine organizational processes and take steps toward preventing unethical conduct before it occurs. Assessments should be made to address a wide variety of possible failures, the seriousness of offense—a violation of fundamental rights and special obligations should receive highest priority—the likelihood of unethical conduct occurring, and the controls in place, if any, to detect unethical conduct if it does in fact occur. Management should then take action to reduce the severity, likelihood of offense, and/or increase the means for detection. Where possible, reducing the severity and likelihood are preferable to increasing the means of detection alone. This approach is similar to Potential Failure Mode and Effects Analysis in quality circles.[18]

- Management should periodically come up with a list of tangible and measurable objectives and initiatives relative to each organizational process and assign responsibility and authority for their actualization. Where possible, management should try to tie or at least relate ethics based objectives and initiatives with financial metrics. Where initiatives are ineffective and when objectives are not met management should make an effort to correct the problem. Some possible measurable objectives metrics are listed below.

  ○ Improving stakeholder perceptions about corporate ethical performance.
  ○ Reducing ethics based complaints relative to particular processes.
  ○ Seeking compliance with recognized environmental and social accountability standards.
  ○ Promoting supplier compliance with recognized environmental and social accountability standards.
  ○ Reducing your company's carbon footprint, environmental impacts, and promoting energy efficiency.
  ○ Tracking the number of human rights violations in your company and down your supply chain.
  ○ Limiting the percentage of operations in areas where human rights violations are prevalent.
  ○ Reducing health and safety incidents in your company and down your supply chain.
  ○ Increasing the hours devoted to ethics training and development.
  ○ Improving social, environmental, intellectual, and human capital in your company and down your supply chain.
  ○ Establishing community involvement projects designed to increase social, environmental, intellectual, and human capital.
  ○ Increasing company diversity.
  ○ Reducing the instances and costs of illegal conduct.

○ Increasing philanthropic donations.
○ Taking formal and informal actions to promote ethical behavior.

As ethics programs are designed to improve character, human resources and development departments ought to play a key role in supporting process level initiatives. This is why we feel that human "resources" requires the additional title of "development." As such, human resources and development should have responsibility and authority to do the following.

- Ensure that employees are aware of and understand the ethics vision statement, codes of conduct, as well as procedures and other documentation. This should not simply be done during initial hiring and then stowed away in a personnel file. Training programs should thus be regularly conducted. Human resources should seek innovative and multimedia forms of marketing to get the message out.
- In addition to awareness training, human resources and development should help develop the ethical reasoning and decision-making capabilities of all employees within an organization (from the lowest to the highest levels on the organizational chart). This will include appropriate forms of stakeholder, utilitarian, and rights based decision-making. It also means helping to cultivate moral sensitivity, imagination, and moral intelligence.[19] Developing and applying an ethical decision-making procedure will foster and provide a standard against which these sorts of attributes can be measured. The steps that should be included in such a procedure are as follows.[20]

○ *Gather the facts.* How did the problem arise? Be a good and thorough detective and obtain all applicable data and information. Reference all appropriate organizational documentation, including the ethics vision statement, codes of conduct, and procedures.

- *Identify all stakeholders.* Identify all potential and mutual stakeholders. Cast a wide net to ensure thorough risk analysis.
- *Identify stakeholder claims.* Think about claims in terms of that which is good, right, and virtuous and identify operative normative judgments.
- *Identify short- and long-term consequences.* Consider the impact of meeting or failing to meet stakeholder claims. Be sure to consider short- and long-term impacts. Managerial decisions should relate consequences to corporate objectives and measures, including impacts on stakeholder satisfaction and short- and long-term financial metrics.
- *Identify obligations to stakeholders.* Highlight obligations grounded in fundamental rights and those that represent special obligations. Fundamental rights and conditions of acute vulnerability and dependence should be given the highest priority; remember that the weakest voice may have the strongest moral claim. Also identify derivative claims, in particular those that relate to an important good. As best as possible define specific positive and negative duties relative to each right.
- *Consider your character and integrity.* What would a virtuous person do? What would you do if you had the courage and support? Organizations have provided role models to help this aspect of decision-making. One of the more popular was at Walt Disney, where when facing a difficult issue executives would ask, "What would Walt do?"
- *Think creatively about potential actions.* Do not limit yourself to shareholders and short-term profitability. Try to engage in moral imagination and examine new possibilities.[21] Seek out advice and look for best practices. Consult with the ethical officer or ethics board, as appropriate. Try to come up with a plan that best drives company success, makes good on fundamental rights and obligations, and best satisfies derivative claims. Where derivative claims and other nonfundamental rights cannot

be immediately met, think about and try to come up with continual improvement measures that would improve the likelihood of meeting such claims in the future.

○ *Form an argument that supports your decision.* Make a decision and provide reasons for your decision. Your decision should be related in the form of an ethical argument. In short, an argument is a set of premises or statements that logically lead to a conclusion. The premises in an ethical argument include certain empirical/descriptive premises or statements and include an appeal to a moral principle or value. Try to use the moral terminology, principles, and values discussed in this book. The following is an example of a simple ethical argument. (1) We ought never to violate fundamental rights. (1a) Fundamental rights protect that which is necessary for human beings to have dignity, integrity, and respect. (1b) Fundamental rights include universal human rights. (2) Forcing employees to stand at their workstation for over 12 hours without a break is consistent with accepted definitions of torture. (3) The right not to be tortured is a human and fundamental right. (4) Therefore, we ought never to force employees to stand for over 12 hours without a break. This sort of argument would then ethically justify taking specific actions to prevent this sort of abuse in practice.

• Ensure that ethical and unethical conduct and ethical character are considered in issues of hiring, firing, promotion, and demotion. There should be performance based rewards for ethical conduct and disincentives for unethical conduct. Human resources and development should create plans for intellectual and moral development.

Continual Improvement

Following Aristotle, becoming an ethical person is an ongoing task that involves trial, error, and a commitment to improvement. In business, the term "continual improvement" refers to a general and systematic

commitment to improve organizational processes and overall performance.[22] At times, improvements may be small, incremental changes,
such as deciding to engage in recycling. At other times, improvement
efforts constitute more encompassing process changes, such as shifting
company mindset to a sustainability paradigm. In any event, the keys to
continual ethical improvement are to build into organizational practices
a degree of honest and critical self-reflection, a tangible commitment to
eliminating the underlying causes of unethical behavior, and the willingness to act on processes in ways to promote ethical conduct. The following suggestions for continual improvement will help build and sustain
an effective ethics program.

- Organizations should conduct periodic ethics audits.
  Similar to gap analyses, ethical audits should be designed
  to determine the degree of compliance to ethics program
  documentation. Audits should also identify opportunities for
  improvement, verify process level and overall effectiveness,
  and identify best practices. A formal audit program should
  be established to help define the audit strategy, develop
  checklists, set the audit flow, and stipulate auditor training
  requirements. Knowledge about quality management system
  auditing philosophy, methods, and techniques will help to
  develop an effective audit program.[23]
- In addition to audits, organizations should implement
  anonymous stakeholder feedback systems for reporting
  unethical conduct. Common feedback systems include ethics
  hotlines and forms of stakeholder satisfaction surveys.
- Organizations should implement a formal system for
  corrective action. Preventive actions are designed to act upon
  processes in order to prevent problems from happening in the
  first place. Corrective actions are designed to act on processes
  to prevent problems from recurring.[24] This is best accomplished by identifying and eliminated the root cause(s) of the
  problem. There are many methods for root cause analysis.[25]
  The most simple, but often effective approach is the "5-Whys"
  method. This method asks problem solvers to ask why (1) the

initial problem occurred, thus determining the immediate and most obvious cause or Why (1). The problem solvers would then ask Why (1) occurred (thus generating Why 2). The problem solvers would then ask Why (2) occurred (thus generating Why 3), and then would repeat the questioning at least two additional times, as appropriate. The end result should be a more rigorous and process oriented change. For example, a seemingly isolated problem involving unethical and illegal purchasing kickbacks may begin with firing the purchasing agent. Further investigation may lead to more systematic changes in hiring and supplier evaluation processes and practices. Problem solvers would then work to eliminate the root cause and take steps to ensure that their actions are effective. Audit results, the results from gap analyses, actual problems that arise from preventive action analysis, and failures to meet process-related and overall organizational objectives all provide opportunities for corrective action.

- Executive managers should conduct comprehensive and periodic reviews of overall ethics program effectiveness. During reviews executive management should:

  ○ Review the ethics vision statement.
  ○ Review process level objectives and associated measurements.
  ○ Review the results of audits and gap analyses.
  ○ Review stakeholder feedback.
  ○ Review corrective and preventive actions.
  ○ Identify things gone right and things gone wrong.
  ○ Determine whether or not the ethics vision statement has been realized.
  ○ Objectively assess the company's overall ethical–organizational culture. The previous bullet points will serve as inputs when making this assessment. There are other psychological and social scientific models that may be employed when assessing the strength of one's organizational culture.[26]

- ○ Come up with corrective actions and an enterprise level action plan for continual improvement.
- ○ Report on ethics program performance. Ethics reporting will help to demonstrate your commitment to the ethics program and will help to measure performance over time. The nature and extent of the report may vary depending on the stakeholder group or groups to which it is addressed. A report should be presented to the governing body. A report should also be prepared and publicly disseminated to all company stakeholders. The Global Reporting Initiative's framework, which focuses on economic, social, and environmental sustainability, provides a useful framework for ethics and sustainability reporting.[27]

Leadership and Discourse

Without question an ethics program will not be effective without leadership at all levels of the organization. All employees must in one sense or another lead by example. Executive managers and governing authorities should openly support the ethics program in word and also by allocating the necessary resources to ensure its effectiveness. Executive management and the board should appoint an ethics officer who has the responsibility and the authority to ensure that the program is effectively documented, implemented, and maintained. Each employee should be aware of ethics program requirements, the company's ethics vision, and demonstrate how they actively promote an ethical organization culture.

There are many leadership models that can help to facilitate these ends, foster ethical conduct, and align with the suggestions of this book. For example, models of cosmopolitan leadership demand, promote, and reward inquisitiveness, learning, critical reflection and deliberation, a sense of belonging and purpose, a sense of mutual recognition and interdependence, and care.[28] Additionally, the transformative leadership model stresses the importance of the leader as a mentor who recognizes individual importance and uniqueness, promotes intellectual stimulation, conveys an overarching vision or purpose that transcends immediate, transactional gain, who acts with the utmost integrity, and ultimately serves as a role model for ethical conduct.[29] Each model, and perhaps many others, helps to align good and effective leadership with the ethics, values, and principles discussed in this book.

Regardless of which leadership model one chooses, leaders will be in situations where they have to maintain integrity during difficult times. As mentioned at several points throughout this book ethical dilemmas and conflict will inevitably occur. One way to deal with conflict is to try and exert strategic influence and through inducements or threats try to advance company interests. The philosopher Jurgen Habermas defines this sort of action as strategic action.[30] There is, of course, a place for strategic action in business. The problem with exerting such an influence, however, is that when strategic actions come to dominate an organizational culture they erode the sense of ethical–organizational integrity outlined here.[31] On the other hand, Habermas defines communicative actions as those attempts to reach mutual understanding and coordinate behavior in terms of a collective assent to the way things ought to be.[32] Different from the disposition to rely on strategic actions, engaging in communicative actions and working toward mutual understanding actually builds solidarity and integrity.[33]

While we should not try to wholly eliminate strategic actions, we should try to foster communicative actions. The way to do this is through discourse. In a debate one party may know very well the position they support and do their best to prove their point. The goal of a debate is to influence opinion in the most effective way possible, sometimes by good, solid argumentation, at other times through purely rhetorical means. Conversely, the goal of discourse is learning and understanding. Participants do not rely on rhetoric or subterfuge but trade arguments in order to find the best reasons for supporting general norms and values over others.[34] At one level, discursive participants should discuss and seek consensus over the guiding values or deep preferences that focus their collective way of life. Using our terminology, mutual stakeholders should engage or otherwise be represented in a discourse about organizational and stakeholder identity and define shared commitments regarding that which is good. At another level, all potential stakeholders should engage or otherwise be represented in a discourse about that which is right or fair. In the end, that which is good and that which is right are not determined by an ethics officer or corporate social responsibility office, but arise out of processes driven toward inclusive stakeholder input and collective recognition. In the end, the results of stakeholder discourse should appropriately shape the organizational ethics vision and other down-level documentation. Several models for incorporating discursive elements in business organizations are suggested in the literature.[35] Some of the general discursive rules to which participants must adhere are as follows.

- A commitment to ethical and moral learning.
- A commitment to recognizing the mutual worth of all participants.
- Willingness to reverse roles and argue and see a position from another's point of view.
- Willingness to give up on one's position when provided good reasons to do so.
- A commitment to represent all stakeholder view and arguments, whether in person or in spirit. Getting all parties in one room might be difficult, but their positions nevertheless could be authentically championed by other constituents.
- Allowing all parties to speak their views and present their positions without retribution.
- A commitment to speaking truthfully and authentically.
- A commitment to finding values and norms that are, or at least would likely be, supported by all those who may be impacted by their recognition.
- A commitment to translate the recognition of said values and norms into practice.
- Without question, discourse is an idealized form of engagement and sometimes difficult to implement in practice. Nevertheless, the ability for leaders to engage in discourse, refrain from threats and inducements, and develop a shared and unifying sense of stakeholder ethical and moral solidarity should be regarded as a central feature of stakeholder management capability.[36]

Conclusion

We began this chapter by recognizing intellectual, cognitive, and motivation limitations to managing for ethical–organizational integrity. An effective ethics program will not eliminate all conflict or eliminate all cases of unethical conduct. An effective program will, however, help to create a culture that will maintain and reaffirm ethical–organizational integrity when cases of ethical conflict or unethical conduct do in fact occur. This integrity is held fast by a commitment to a systematic and process oriented approach to intellectual and moral development. To reiterate a crucial point, ethics is not merely about applying discrete rules or seeking minimal compliance. Ethics is about transforming ourselves and our practices to reflect higher ideals about that which is ultimately good and right.

Questions for Further Research and Discussion

Can you provide concrete examples and best cases of ethics program effectiveness?

Why do some ethics programs fail?

What are some of the impediments to promoting an ethical organizational culture?

What are some of the impediments to ethical decision-making?

What are some of the variables that determine moral sensitivity, awareness, and impact ethical decision-making?

What psychological and social scientific models can best assess organizational culture?

What leadership models best promote ethical–organizational integrity?

Are there any ethical conflict resolution models that work better than others?

Conclusion

For some time people thought that business and ethics constituted separate and mutually exclusive realms. Those who hold such a belief or still maintain that "business ethics" is somehow an oxymoron do so at their own risk. Indeed, the recent failures in the financial industries that precipitated the financial crises we are still dealing with illustrate the systematic dangers to companies, investors, and the public that stem from attempts to engage in business in a moral vacuum. Business presupposes a moral foundation and requires an ethical framework if it is to serve the very real needs that it is designed to fulfill in society. From what we have learned, behaving ethically in business and promoting ethical–organizational integrity and long-term company success are intimately related and mutually dependent.

For those philosophers who have devoted their attention to economics and business and society, as well as to astute businesspersons this should come as no real surprise. Indeed, the principles and values prescribed by the great ethicists are shared by companies who are, so to speak, "built to last."[1] While profit and money may be important goods, ethical philosophers and reflective businesspersons would argue that the key to success in life and in business involves higher standards than those grounded in the unrestrained pursuit of immediate interests. Philosophers and the top business thinkers are visionaries. They are not satisfied with the way things are but continually try to envision and actualize the way things ought to be. Their goals are both big and audacious. Doing well enough is fine, but we ought to be committed to bringing about states of affairs that *best* promote and maximize happiness and company success. This requires innovation, imagination, and creativity. In seeking to best drive company success we must likewise be committed to *always* respecting the humanity and dignity of all stakeholders. We should not simply satisfy our immediate desires but strive to be virtuous, *flourish* as individuals and organizations, and live up to our *greatest potential*. We must realize that living up to these ideals is difficult and requires work, practice, trial and error, improvement, and courage. Although difficult, these commitments will help define a core moral ideology that defines who we are and what we stand for as an organization of businesspersons. Those who align themselves with the values and principles defined therein are aligned with a higher purpose and conviction. While businesses come and go, it is thus the ethical value and principles upon which organizations are founded that ought to be built to last. And this is the vision that will sustain both the future of business and a society that can best promote the goods that businesses can provide for persons in those societies.

This of course does not mean that managers and other employees will not face very difficult situations and encounter ethical dilemmas and conflicts. At times the path that best promotes and maximizes long-term value will be unclear. At times powerful individuals or stakeholder groups may try to influence behavior that is perhaps unethical or does not align with long-term company success. At times there will be situations where leaders may know the right thing to do on principle but fail to understand how to best realize it. At other times stakeholders in and outside your organization may fail to abide by the most basic moral prohibitions and violate fundamental rights and opportunistically exploit the most vulnerable and dependent. No book, ethical theory, or managerial approach will prevent such things from occurring. Optimally dealing with these sorts of difficult ethical issues in business requires moral sophistication and a firm commitment to systematically bringing ethics into management systems and organizational processes. Business is not separate from ethics, nor does a business ethic merely impose constraints on business practices. As stated at various points throughout this work, being ethical in business involves trying to transform ourselves, our practices, and our organizations to better and continually reflect higher normative ideals. No framework will guarantee business success. What our framework will do, however, is to help ensure that whether we succeed or fail in business, we do so with integrity.

APPENDIX A

Ford Motor Company's Code of Basic Working Conditions

This Code of Basic Working Conditions represents the commitment of Ford and its worldwide subsidiaries. The diverse group of men and women who work for Ford are our most important resource. In recognition of their contributions, we have developed policies and programs designed to ensure that our employees enjoy the protection afforded by the principles articulated today in this Code. While these principles are not new to Ford, they are vitally important to what we stand for as a company. Consequently, we have chosen to summarize them here in an expression of our global commitment.

While this Code of Conduct serves to detail, specifically, our standards for labor and environmental standards throughout our global operations, it also stands as a general endorsement of the following human rights frameworks and charters:

- The UN Universal Declaration of Human Rights
- The ILO Tripartite Declaration of Principles concerning Multinational Enterprises and Social Policy
- OECD Guidelines for Multinational Enterprises
- The Global Sullivan Principles of Social Responsibility

The diverse universe in which Ford operates requires that a Code such as this be general in nature. In certain situations, local legal requirements, collective bargaining agreements, and agreements freely entered into by employees may supersede portions of this Code. Nevertheless, we believe this Code affirms important, universal values that serve as the cornerstone of our relationship with employees.

Child Labor

We will not use child labor. In no event will we employ any person below the age of 15, unless this is part of a government-authorized job training or apprenticeship program that would be clearly beneficial to the persons participating.

Compensation

We will promote our employees' material well-being by providing compensation and benefits that are competitive and comply with applicable law.

Forced Labor

We will not use forced labor, regardless of its form. We will not tolerate physically abusive disciplinary practices.

Freedom of Association and Collective Bargaining

We recognize and respect our employees' right to associate freely and bargain collectively. We will work constructively with recognized representatives to promote the interests of our employees. In locations where employees are not represented by unions, we will seek to provide opportunities for employee concerns to be heard.

Harassment and Discrimination

We will not tolerate harassment or discrimination on the basis of sex, race, color, creed, religion, age, ethnic or national origin, marital/parental status, pregnancy, disability, sexual orientation, or veteran status.

Health and Safety

We will provide and maintain for all employees a safe and healthy working environment that meets or exceeds applicable standards for occupational safety and health.

Work Hours

We will comply with applicable law regulating hours of work.

Community Engagement and Indigenous Populations

We shall consider indigenous peoples among our primary stakeholders in all projects we consider undertaking. We will openly and honestly engage all recognized members of our stakeholder community who have an interest in our activities.

Bribery and Corruption

We will under no circumstances tolerate the giving or receiving of undue reward to influence the behavior of another individual, organization, politician, or government body, so as to acquire a commercial advantage; this extends to all of our regional operations, regardless of whether bribery is officially tolerated and condoned.

Environment and Sustainability

We will conduct business in an environmentally friendly and responsible manner. We will seek to reduce and minimize the environmental impact of all of our operations in the short term, as we seek to become an environmentally restorative and truly sustainable company in the long term.

Responsibility and Implementation

We will communicate this Code of Basic Working Conditions to all employees. As appropriate under local practice, we will seek the support and assistance of unions and employee representatives in this effort. We will encourage our business partners throughout our value chain to adopt and enforce similar policies. We will seek to identify and utilize business partners who aspire in the conduct of their business to standards that are consistent with this Code.

Employees with a good-faith belief that there may have been a violation of this Code should report it through established channels, if known, or to the Office of the General Counsel. No retaliatory actions will be taken against any employee who makes such a report or cooperates in an investigation of such a violation reported by someone else.

Verification

We will, as appropriate, seek the assistance of independent third parties to verify our compliance with this Code.

APPENDIX B

APSC Capability Checklist

Principles	Elements	Checklist
1 Align learning with the business	Agency capability requirements	Do learning and development strategies and plans reflect agency capability requirements against business outcomes as identified in corporate planning documents?
		Are agency capability requirements identified and articulated in people management/workforce plans?
	Governance	Does the organization have a structured and accountable approach to the management of learning and development?
	Agency culture	Are processes in place to map the agency's culture against the desired culture and do learning and development plans and strategies reflect cultural realities and goals?
	Funding mechanisms and processes	Are learning and development strategies sufficiently and appropriately funded for short- and long-term future needs?
2 Integrate learning with HR and other business processes	Other people management strategies and plans	Are there mechanisms in place to ensure that all people management strategies are coherent?
	People management processes	Do employees know and understand the agency's capability requirements?
		Are managers and employees aware of their roles and responsibilities regarding individual development and career management?
	Agency core business processes	Is learning and development considered a legitimate part of day-to-day business?
		Are existing business processes and forums used to advance learning and development goals?

(*Continued*)

Principles	Elements	Checklist
	HR Management Information Systems (HRMIS)	Is there a system that provides for the collection and reporting of minimum baseline data, which is integrated with agency management information systems?
3 Create a learning culture	Leading by example	Are senior and line managers creating a positive work environment, modelling learning for themselves and supporting learning and development in the agency?
	Active commitment	Is there appropriate promotion, recognition and resourcing of learning and development by senior management?
	Blurring the lines between learning and work	Do managers see learning and development as a legitimate and valued workplace activity?
4 Provide appropriate learning options	Needs-based content	Are learning and development options based on organizational, business unit and individual priorities and needs?
	Appropriate interventions	Are learning and development options cost-effective, relevant, and action-oriented to facilitate transfer of learning to the workplace?
		Are learning and development options varied, timely, flexible, collaborative, and compatible with individual learning styles and adult learning principles?
5 Manage learning effectively	Value for money service delivery	Do you know that your learning and development function is delivering value for money?
	Effective stakeholder relationships	Are stakeholder relationships with staff, managers, service providers, executive, Parliament effective?
	Monitoring and reporting	Are there systems in place to monitor and report on learning and development activities?
6 Support application of skills in the workplace	Supportive workplace environment	Are mentoring and coaching by managers on the job a part of learning and development in the agency?
	Opportunities to apply new skills	Are there incentives in place to ensure that line managers encourage and provide opportunities to test and develop new skills?

(Continued)

(Continued)

Principles	Elements	Checklist
	Opportunities to disseminate new knowledge	Are there support and assistance systems available to advise and support managers and individuals in identified capability areas?
		Are staff encouraged to share learning in specific subject matter/specialist areas through knowledge networks?
	On-the-job performance evaluation	Do staff and managers translate performance management activities into development action plans?
7 Evaluate learning and development	Relevance	Do learning and development investments address business, capability and individual needs?
	Appropriateness	Are learning and development investments appropriate in terms of time, cost, quality, and integration with other strategies and practices?
	Reaction	Are learners satisfied with the accessibility and quality of learning and development?
	Capability acquired	Have learning and development improved individual and agency knowledge, skills, and competency?
	Performance on the job	Has learning been transferred to the workplace?
	Outcomes	Do you assess the outcomes of learning and development?

APPENDIX C

International Code of Ethics for Sales and Marketing

1. **I hereby acknowledge** my accountability to the organization for which I work and to society as a whole to improve sales knowledge and practice and to adhere to the highest professional standards in my work and personal relationships.
2. **My concept of selling** includes as its basic principle the sovereignty of all consumers in the marketplace and the necessity for mutual benefit to both buyer and seller in all transactions.
3. **I shall personally maintain** the highest standards of ethical and professional conduct in all my business relationships with customers, suppliers, colleagues, competitors, governmental agencies, and the public.
4. **I pledge to protect**, support, and promote the principles of consumer choice, competition, and innovation enterprise, consistent with relevant legislative public policy standards.
5. **I shall not knowingly participate** in actions, agreements, or marketing policies or practices which may be detrimental to customers, competitors, or established community social or economic policies or standards.
6. **I shall strive to ensure** that products and services are distributed through such channels and by such methods as will tend to optimize the distributive process by offering maximum customer value and service at minimum cost while providing fair and equitable compensation for all parties.
7. **I shall support efforts** to increase productivity or reduce costs of production or marketing through standardization or other methods, provided these methods do not stifle innovation or creativity.

8. **I believe prices** should reflect true value in use of the product or service to the customer, including the pricing of goods and services transferred among operating organizations worldwide.

9. **I acknowledge** that providing the best economic and social product value consistent with cost also includes: (a) recognizing the customer's right to expect safe products with clear instructions for their proper use and maintenance; (b) providing easily accessible channels for customer complaints; (c) investigating any customer dissatisfaction objectively and taking prompt and appropriate remedial action; (d) recognizing and supporting proven public policy objectives such as conserving energy and protecting the environment.

10. **I pledge my efforts** to assure that all marketing research, advertising, and presentations of products, services, or concepts are done clearly, truthfully, and in good taste so as not to mislead or offend customers. I further pledge to assure that all these activities are conducted in accordance with the highest standards of each profession and generally accepted principles of fair competition.

11. **I pledge to cooperate** fully in furthering the efforts of all institutions, media, professional associations, and other organizations to publicize this creed as widely as possible throughout the world.

APPENDIX D

Universal Declaration of Human Rights*

Article 1.

All human beings are born free and equal in dignity and rights. They are endowed with reason and conscience and should act toward one another in a spirit of brotherhood.

Article 2.

Everyone is entitled to all the rights and freedoms set forth in this Declaration, without distinction of any kind, such as race, color, sex, language, religion, political or other opinion, national or social origin, property, birth or other status. Furthermore, no distinction shall be made on the basis of the political, jurisdictional or international status of the country or territory to which a person belongs, whether it be independent, trust, non-self-governing or under any other limitation of sovereignty.

Article 3.

Everyone has the right to life, liberty and security of person.

Article 4.

No one shall be held in slavery or servitude; slavery and the slave trade shall be prohibited in all their forms.

Article 5.

No one shall be subjected to torture or to cruel, inhuman or degrading treatment or punishment.

Article 6.

Everyone has the right to recognition everywhere as a person before the law.

---

*Source: Courtesy Universal Declaration of Human Rights.

Article 7.

All are equal before the law and are entitled without any discrimination to equal protection of the law. All are entitled to equal protection against any discrimination in violation of this Declaration and against any incitement to such discrimination.

Article 12.

No one shall be subjected to arbitrary interference with his privacy, family, home or correspondence, nor to attacks upon his honor and reputation. Everyone has the right to the protection of the law against such interference or attacks.

Article 17.

1. Everyone has the right to own property alone as well as in association with others.
2. No one shall be arbitrarily deprived of his property.

Article 18.

Everyone has the right to freedom of thought, conscience and religion; this right includes freedom to change his religion or belief, and freedom, either alone or in community with others and in public or private, to manifest his religion or belief in teaching, practice, worship and observance.

Article 19.

Everyone has the right to freedom of opinion and expression; this right includes freedom to hold opinions without interference and to seek, receive and impart information and ideas through any media and regardless of frontiers.

Article 20.

1. Everyone has the right to freedom of peaceful assembly and association.
2. No one may be compelled to belong to an association.

Article 22.

Everyone, as a member of society, has the right to social security and is entitled to realization, through national effort and international co-operation and in accordance with the organization and resources of each

State, of the economic, social and cultural rights indispensable for his dignity and the free development of his personality.

Article 23.

1. Everyone has the right to work, to free choice of employment, to just and favorable conditions of work and to protection against unemployment.
2. Everyone, without any discrimination, has the right to equal pay for equal work.
3. Everyone who works has the right to just and favorable remuneration ensuring for himself and his family an existence worthy of human dignity, and supplemented, if necessary, by other means of social protection.
4. Everyone has the right to form and to join trade unions for the protection of his interests.

Article 24.

Everyone has the right to rest and leisure, including reasonable limitation of working hours and periodic holidays with pay.

Article 25.

1. Everyone has the right to a standard of living adequate for the health and well-being of himself and of his family, including food, clothing, housing and medical care and necessary social services, and the right to security in the event of unemployment, sickness, disability, widowhood, old age or other lack of livelihood in circumstances beyond his control.
2. Motherhood and childhood are entitled to special care and assistance. All children, whether born in or out of wedlock, shall enjoy the same social protection.

Article 26.

1. Everyone has the right to education.
2. Education shall be directed to the full development of the human personality and to the strengthening of respect for human rights and fundamental freedoms.

APPENDIX E

Shareholder Key Rights as Identified by the OECD*

The corporate governance framework should protect and facilitate the exercise of shareholders' rights.

A. Basic shareholder rights should include the right to: 1) secure methods of ownership registration; 2) convey or transfer shares; 3) obtain relevant and material information on the corporation on a timely and regular basis; 4) participate and vote in general shareholder meetings; 5) elect and remove members of the board; and 6) share in the profits of the corporation.

B. Shareholders should have the right to participate in, and to be sufficiently informed on, decisions concerning fundamental corporate changes such as: 1) amendments to the statutes, or articles of incorporation or similar governing documents of the company; 2) the authorization of additional shares; and 3) extraordinary transactions, including the transfer of all or substantially all assets, that in effect result in the sale of the company.

C. Shareholders should have the opportunity to participate effectively and vote in general shareholder meetings and should be informed of the rules, including voting procedures, that govern general shareholder meetings:

1. Shareholders should be furnished with sufficient and timely information concerning the date, location and agenda of general meetings, as well as full and timely information regarding the issues to be decided at the meeting.
2. Shareholders should have the opportunity to ask questions to the board, including questions relating to the annual external audit, to place items on the agenda of general meetings, and to propose resolutions, subject to reasonable limitations.

---

*Source: Courtesy Shareholder Key Rights as Identified by the OECD.

3. Effective shareholder participation in key corporate governance decisions, such as the nomination and election of board members, should be facilitated. Shareholders should be able to make their views known on the remuneration policy for board members and key executives. The equity component of compensation schemes for board members and employees should be subject to shareholder approval.

4. Shareholders should be able to vote in person or in absentia, and equal effect should be given to votes whether cast in person or in absentia.

D. Capital structures and arrangements that enable certain shareholders to obtain a degree of control disproportionate to their equity ownership should be disclosed.

E. Markets for corporate control should be allowed to function in an efficient and transparent manner.

1. The rules and procedures governing the acquisition of corporate control in the capital markets, and extraordinary transactions such as mergers, and sales of substantial portions of corporate assets, should be clearly articulated and disclosed so that investors understand their rights and recourse. Transactions should occur at transparent prices and under fair conditions that protect the rights of all shareholders according to their class.

2. Anti-take-over devices should not be used to shield management and the board from accountability.

F. The exercise of ownership rights by all shareholders, including institutional investors, should be facilitated.

1. Institutional investors acting in a fiduciary capacity should disclose their overall corporate governance and voting policies with respect to their investments, including the procedures that they have in place for deciding on the use of their voting rights.

2. Institutional investors acting in a fiduciary capacity should disclose how they manage material conflicts of interest that may affect the exercise of key ownership rights regarding their investments.

G. Shareholders, including institutional shareholders, should be allowed to consult with each other on issues concerning their basic shareholder rights as defined in the Principles, subject to exceptions to prevent abuse.

Sarbanes Oxley Summary

Summary of Section 302

Periodic statutory financial reports are to include certifications that:

- The signing officers have reviewed the report
- The report does not contain any material untrue statements or material omission or be considered misleading
- The financial statements and related information fairly present the financial condition and the results in all material respects
- The signing officers are responsible for internal controls and have evaluated these internal controls within the previous ninety days and have reported on their findings
- A list of all deficiencies in the internal controls and information on any fraud that involves employees who are involved with internal activities
- Any significant changes in internal controls or related factors that could have a negative impact on the internal controls

Organizations may not attempt to avoid these requirements by reincorporating their activities or transferring their activities outside of the United States.

Summary of Section 401

Financial statements published by issuers are required to be accurate and presented in a manner that does not contain incorrect statements or admit to state material information. These financial statements shall also include all material off-balance sheet liabilities, obligations or transactions. The Commission was required to study and report on the extent of off-balance transactions resulting transparent reporting. The Commission is also required to determine whether generally accepted accounting principals or other regulations result in open and meaningful reporting by issuers.

Summary of Section 404

Issuers are required to publish information in their annual reports concerning the scope and adequacy of the internal control structure and procedures for financial reporting. This statement shall also assess the effectiveness of such internal controls and procedures.

The registered accounting firm shall, in the same report, attest to and report on the assessment on the effectiveness of the internal control structure and procedures for financial reporting.

Summary of Section 409

Issuers are required to disclose to the public, on an urgent basis, information on material changes in their financial condition or operations. These disclosures are to be presented in terms that are easy to understand supported by trend and qualitative information of graphic presentations as appropriate.

Summary of Section 802

This section imposes penalties of fines and/or up to 20 years imprisonment for altering, destroying, mutilating, concealing, falsifying records, documents or tangible objects with the intent to obstruct, impede or influence a legal investigation. This section also imposes penalties of fines and/or imprisonment up to 10 years on any accountant who knowingly and willfully violates the requirements of maintenance of all audit or review papers for a period of 5 years.

APPENDIX F

U.S. Federal Sentencing Guidelines—Chapter 8

§8B2.1. Effective Compliance and Ethics Program

a. To have an effective compliance and ethics program ... an organization shall—

   1. exercise due diligence to prevent and detect criminal conduct; and

   2. otherwise promote an organizational culture that encourages ethical conduct and a commitment to compliance with the law.

Such compliance and ethics program shall be reasonably designed, implemented, and enforced so that the program is generally effective in preventing and detecting criminal conduct. The failure to prevent or detect the instant offense does not necessarily mean that the program is not generally effective in preventing and detecting criminal conduct.

b. Due diligence and the promotion of an organizational culture that encourages ethical conduct and a commitment to compliance with the law within the meaning of subsection (a) minimally require the following:

   1. The organization shall establish standards and procedures to prevent and detect criminal conduct.

   2. (A) The organization's governing authority shall be knowledgeable about the content and operation of the compliance and ethics program and shall exercise reasonable oversight with respect to the implementation and effectiveness of the compliance and ethics program.

   (B) High-level personnel of the organization shall ensure that the organization has an effective compliance and ethics program, as described in this guideline. Specific individual(s) within high-level personnel shall be assigned overall responsibility for the compliance and ethics program.

(C) Specific individual(s) within the organization shall be delegated day-to-day operational responsibility for the compliance and ethics program. Individual(s) with operational responsibility shall report periodically to high-level personnel and, as appropriate, to the governing authority, or an appropriate subgroup of the governing authority, on the effectiveness of the compliance and ethics program. To carry out such operational responsibility, such individual(s) shall be given adequate resources, appropriate authority, and direct access to the governing authority or an appropriate subgroup of the governing authority.

3. The organization shall use reasonable efforts not to include within the substantial authority personnel of the organization any individual whom the organization knew, or should have known through the exercise of due diligence, has engaged in illegal activities or other conduct inconsistent with an effective compliance and ethics program.

4. (A) The organization shall take reasonable steps to communicate periodically and in a practical manner its standards and procedures, and other aspects of the compliance and ethics program, to the individuals referred to in subparagraph (B) by conducting effective training programs and otherwise disseminating information appropriate to such individuals' respective roles and responsibilities.

(B) The individuals referred to in subparagraph (A) are the members of the governing authority, high-level personnel, substantial authority personnel, the organization's employees, and, as appropriate, the organization's agents.

5. The organization shall take reasonable steps—

(A) to ensure that the organization's compliance and ethics program is followed, including monitoring and auditing to detect criminal conduct;

(B) to evaluate periodically the effectiveness of the organization's compliance and ethics program; and

(C) to have and publicize a system, which may include mechanisms that allow for anonymity or confidentiality, whereby the organization's employees and agents may report or seek guidance regarding potential or actual criminal conduct without fear of retaliation.

6. The organization's compliance and ethics program shall be promoted and enforced consistently throughout the organization through (A) appropriate incentives to perform in accordance with the compliance and ethics program; and (B) appropriate disciplinary measures for engaging in criminal conduct and for failing to take reasonable steps to prevent or detect criminal conduct.

7. After criminal conduct has been detected, the organization shall take reasonable steps to respond appropriately to the criminal conduct and to prevent further similar criminal conduct, including making any necessary modifications to the organization's compliance and ethics program.

c. In implementing subsection (b), the organization shall periodically assess the risk of criminal conduct and shall take appropriate steps to design, implement, or modify each requirement set forth in subsection (b) to reduce the risk of criminal conduct identified through this process.

APPENDIX G

Johnson & Johnson Credo*

We believe our first responsibility is to the doctors, nurses and patients, to mothers and fathers and all others who use our products and services. In meeting their needs everything we do must be of high quality.

We must constantly strive to reduce our costs in order to maintain reasonable prices. Customers' orders must be serviced promptly and accurately. Our suppliers and distributors must have an opportunity to make a fair profit.

We are responsible to our employees, the men and women who work with us throughout the world. Everyone must be considered as an individual. We must respect their dignity and recognize their merit. They must have a sense of security in their jobs.

Compensation must be fair and adequate, and working conditions clean, orderly and safe. We must be mindful of ways to help our employees fulfill their family responsibilities.

Employees must feel free to make suggestions and complaints. There must be equal opportunity for employment, development and advancement for those qualified.

We must provide competent management, and their actions must be just and ethical.

We are responsible to the communities in which we live and work and to the world community as well. We must be good citizens – support good works and charities and bear our fair share of taxes. We must encourage civic improvements and better health and education.

We must maintain in good order the property we are privileged to use, protecting the environment and natural resources.

Our final responsibility is to our stockholders. Business must make a sound profit. We must experiment with new ideas. Research must be carried on, innovative programs developed and mistakes paid for.

---

*Source: Courtesy Johnson and Johnson Credo.

New equipment must be purchased, new facilities provided and new products launched. Reserves must be created to provide for adverse times. When we operate according to these principles, the stockholders should realize a fair return.

Novartis Commitment to Human Rights*

At Novartis we believe that respect for human rights is sound business practice. As a responsible corporate citizen, we aim to exert an enlightened presence wherever we operate.

Human rights apply to all people throughout the world. They should guarantee everyone, everywhere, a life in freedom and dignity.

Novartis considers that upholding human rights is fundamental to sustainable social and economic development. We fully support the protection of such rights as enshrined in the United Nations' Universal Declaration of Human Rights (UDHR).

Human rights are cross-cutting issues affecting all aspects of our business, from research and development and clinical trials to marketing and the pricing of medicines. In addition to rights, such as labor norms, which hold the same relevance for all companies, there are rights of particular significance to the pharmaceutical sector, such as the right to medical care, sometimes referred to as the right to health. We are engaged in partnerships with public and private sector organizations to respond to global health challenges by exploring approaches such as tiered pricing, donations and capacity-building.

Novartis has a longstanding commitment to human rights. We were among the first signatories of the United Nations Global Compact in 2000. As early as 2003, we were among the few multinational corporations to have developed a guideline on human rights which sets out our commitments and responsibilities in this area.

Novartis was a founding member of the Business Leaders Initiative on Human Rights (BLIHR) and has made a major contribution to furthering collective understanding of the role of business in respecting and upholding human rights.

*Source: Courtesy Novartis AG.

As well as ensuring that we are not complicit in human rights violations, we support human rights by adopting a proactive, "rights-aware" approach across all of our businesses. Through the think tank work of the Novartis Foundation for Sustainable Development, we are helping to define the part business can play in promoting human rights in general and the right to health in particular.

In addition, since 2006, we have been collaborating with the Danish Institute for Human Rights to develop a version of their Human Rights Compliance Assessment tool adapted to the pharmaceutical industry. We are also involved in pioneering efforts to apply the concept of a living wage across our worldwide operations.

Texas Instruments Ethics and Value Statement*

Ethics is the Cornerstone of TI

Our reputation at TI depends upon all of the decisions we make and all the actions we take personally each day. Our values define how we will evaluate our decisions and actions and how we will conduct our business. We are working in a difficult, demanding, ever-changing business environment. Together, we are building a work environment on the foundation of integrity, innovation and commitment.

Together, we are moving our company into a new century one good decision at a time. Our high standards have rewarded us with an enviable reputation in today's marketplace: a reputation of integrity, honesty and trustworthiness. That strong ethical reputation is a vital asset, and each of us shares a personal responsibility to protect, preserve and enhance it. Our reputation is a strong, but silent partner in all business relationships. By understanding and applying the values presented here, each of us can say to ourselves and to others, "TI is a good company and one reason is that I am a part of it."

Know what's right. Value what's right. Do what's right.

---

*Source: Courtesy Texas Instruments.

Integrity

- We exercise the basic virtues of respect, dignity, kindness, courtesy and manners in all work relationships.
- We recognize and avoid behaviors that others may find offensive, including the manner in which we speak and relate to one another and the materials we bring into the workplace, both printed and electronically.
- We respect the right and obligation of every TIer to resolve concerns relating to ethics questions without retribution and retaliation.
- We give all TIers the same opportunity to have their questions, issues and situations fairly considered, while understanding that being treated fairly does not always mean that we will all be treated the same.
- We trust one another to use sound judgment in our use of TI business and information systems.
- We understand that even though TI has the obligation to monitor its business information systems activity, we will respect privacy by prohibiting random searches of individual TIers' communications.

Innovation

- We recognize that conduct socially and professionally acceptable in one culture and country may be viewed differently.
- We work together with trust to achieve superior results.
- We hire, promote and reward individuals without regard to race, color, religion, creed, disability, national origin, gender, gender identity and expression, age, sexual orientation, marital status, or veteran status.
- We encourage open, honest and candid communications.
- We maintain a professional work environment that is both satisfying and rewarding.
- We give recognition and credit appropriately and frequently.
- We respect all TIers without regard to their position or level within the organization.

We understand that working together successfully may depend upon our willingness to trust someone else to take the lead.

- We strive to win aggressively and do so with the highest standards of ethics.
- We take responsible risks, managing those risks and learning from our experiences.
- We promote workplace flexibility to make TI the employer of choice for the most creative and innovative people.
- We seek out new perspectives and ideas through a diverse work force.
- We recognize that we succeed or fail together.

Commitment

- We keep our skills current and competitive by taking the initiative for our personal development.
- We take full accountability for our actions and responsibility for the outcome.
- We protect TI's reputation for integrity in all business dealings.
- We make a difference to our customers, our suppliers, one another, our communities and society.
- We set high standards of personal performance and professional growth.
- We take personal pride in what we do.
- We stay committed to results.
- We listen to our customers and meet or exceed their expectations.
- We seek to understand, value and leverage our diverse cultural differences and perspectives.

Notes

Introduction

1. United States Sentencing Commission (2010).
2. Palmer and Zakhem (2001).
3. R-BEC (2001).
4. OECD (2011).
5. Solomon (1997).
6. Orlitzky, Schmidt, and Rynes (2003).
7. Bassi, Frauenheim, and McMurrer et al. (2011).
8. Quoted in Laszlo (2008), p. 14.
9. Rachels and Rachels (2011).
10. Paine (1994).
11. Friedman (September 13th, 1970).
12. Donaldson (2005).
13. DesJardins (2005).

Chapter 1

1. Carroll (1999).
2. Friedman (1970).
3. Mill (2001).
4. Friedman (1970).
5. Ibid.
6. Sandberg (2008a), (2008b); Wempe (2008); Freeman (2008), (1994).
7. DesJardins and McCall (2005), pp. 34–43.
8. Sen (2009), (2005), (1993); Nussbaum (2000).
9. Jensen (2002).
10. Porter, Lorsch, and Nohria (2004).
11. Kaplan and Norton (1996), p. 76.
12. Dowie (1997).
13. Birsch and Fielder (1994).
14. Bazerman and Tenbrunsel (2011).
15. Martin (2010).
16. Verschoor (1998).
17. Freeman (2008).
18. Ford Motor Company (2010/2011).

19. Laszlo (2008).
20. Capital One (2012).
21. DesJardins (2005), p. 17.
22. DesJardins (2005).
23. Jensen (2002).
24. Jensen (2002).
25. Donaldson and Preston (1995).
26. Abrams (1951).
27. Ackoff (1970); Dill (1975).
28. Freeman (1984).
29. Phillips, Freeman, and Wicks (2003).
30. Argandona (1998).
31. Bowie (1998b).
32. Burton and Dunn (1996); Wicks, Gilbert, and Freeman (1994).
33. Zakhem (2008); Reed (1999).
34. Freeman (2008).
35. Phillips (1997).
36. Freeman and Phillips (2002)
37. Vos (2003); Phillips (2003); Kaler (2002); Clarkson (1998); Mitchell, Agle, and Wood (1997); Starik (1995).
38. Marcoux (2003); Marens and Wick (1999); Goodpaster and Holloran (1994); Goodpaster (1991).
39. Freeman, Harrison, Wick, Parmar, de Colle (2010); Jensen (2000).
40. Freeman et al. 2010.
41. Freeman (1994).
42. Aristotle (1962).
43. George (2003).
44. Fukuyama (1994), p. 26.
45. National Association of Corporate Directors (2012).
46. Sen (2009), (2005), (1993); Nussbaum (2000).
47. Renouard (2011); Bertland (2009).
48. Valentine, Godkin, and Fleischman (2011).
49. Benford, Bowers, Fahlen, Mariani, and Rodden (1994).
50. APSC (2002).
51. Phillips et al. (2003).
52. Freeman (1994).

Chapter 2

1. Friedman (1970).
2. Stout (2002).

3. DesJardins and McCall (2005), pp. 16–20.
4. Freeman, Wicks, and Parmar (2004), p. 365.
5. Carroll (1991).
6. Kant (1998).
7. Habermas (1987), pp. 119–152.
8. Donaldson (2005).
9. UN General Assembly (1948).
10. DesJardins and McCall (2005), p. 53.
11. Rachels (1975).
12. Lippke (1989); DesJardins (1987); Brenkert (1981).
13. Donaldson (2005), pp. 482–488.
14. DesJardins (2005).
15. DesJardins (2005).
16. Goodin (1985), pp. 195–196.
17. Marcoux (2003).
18. Arnold and Bowie (2003).
19. DesJardins (2005).
20. OECD (2011); *Sarbanes Oxley Act* (2002).
21. Donaldson (2005).
22. Arnold and Bowie (2003).
23. Bowie (1998a).
24. Great Place to Work (2011).
25. Kimberly-Clark (2012).
26. Werhane (2005).
27. Barry (2007).
28. Brenkert (2000).
29. McCall (2005).
30. Arnold and Bowie (2003).
31. Cohan (2001).

Chapter 3

1. Aristotle (1962).
2. Ibid, pp. 14–19.
3. Ibid, pp. 48–49.
4. Ibid, pp. 41–44.
5. Ibid, pp. 68–77.
6. Ibid, pp. 83–89.
7. Ibid, p. 32.
8. Ibid, pp. 33–35.
9. Jackall (1988).

10. BB&T (2012).
11. Werhane (2002); Paine (1994).
12. Ferrell, LeClair, and Ferrell (1998); Rafalko (1994).
13. Palmer and Zakhem (2001); Izraeli and Schwartz (1998); Jackson (1997).
14. Michaelson (2006); Laufer (2006); Arjoon (2005); Reynolds and Bowie (2004); McKendall, DeMarr, and Jones-Rickers (2002); Trevino and Nelson (1999).
15. Hess (2007), p. 1792.
16. United Stated Sentencing Commission (2010), section 2.C(ii).
17. ISO (2008); Quality Management Principles (2001).
18. Tague (2005).
19. Colle and Werhane (2000); Pedersen (2009); Werhane (1999); Werhane (2002).
20. Trevino and Nelson (1999), pp. 85–90.
21. Werhane (2002).
22. Deming (1986).
23. Kausek (2006).
24. International Organization for Standardization (2001).
25. Kausek (2006).
26. Kaptein (2008a), (2008b); Kaptein and Avelino (2005); Loe, Ferrell, and Mansfield (2000).
27. GRI http://www.globalreporting.org/NR/rdonlyres/D8B503A9-070C-43DB-AD0F-5C4ACB1EBF39/0/G31RefSheet.pdf
28. Pless and Maak (2008).
29. Bass and Steidlmeier (1999); Bass (1994); Burns (1978).
30. Habermas (1990), p. 58.
31. Habermas (1987), pp. 140–143.
32. Habermas (1984), pp. 94–96.
33. Habermas (1987), pp. 119–152.
34. Habermas (1993), p. 23, (1990), p. 65.
35. Stansbury (2009); Zakhem (2008); Reynolds and Yuthas (2008); Palazzo and Scherer (2006); Gilbert and Rasche (2007); Reed (1999).
36. Zakhem (2008).

Conclusion

1. Collins and Porras (1994).

References

Abrams, F. (1951). Management responsibilities in a complex world. *Harvard Business Review 29*(5), 29–34.

Ackoff, R. (1970). *A concept of corporate planning.* New York, NY: John Wiley and Sons.

Argandona, A. (1998). The stakeholder theory and the common good. *Journal of Business Ethics 17*(9), 1093–1102.

Aristotle (1962). *Nicomachean Ethics.* Translated by M. Ostwald. New York, NY: Macmillan Publishing.

Arjoon, S. (2005). Corporate governance: An ethical perspective. *Journal of Business Ethics 61*, 343–352.

Arnold, D., & Bowie, N. (2003). Sweatshops and respect for persons. *Business Ethics Quarterly 13*(2), 221–242.

APSC (2002). *Building corporate capability: The APS in transition.* Retrieved January 5, 2012, from Australian Public Service Commission: www.apsc.gov.au/publications00/benchmarking.htm

Barry, B. (2007). *Speechless: The erosion of free speech in the American workplace.* San Francisco, CA: Berrett-Koehler Publishers.

Bass, B. (1994). *Improving organizational effectiveness through transformational leadership.* Thousand Oaks, CA: Sage Publications.

Bass, B., & Steidlmeier, P. (1999). Ethics, character, and authentic transformational leadership behavior. *The Leadership Quarterly 10*, 181–217.

Bassi, L., Frauenheim, E, & McMurrer, D. (2011). *Good company: Business success in the worthiness era.* San Francisco, CA: Berrett-Koehler Publishers, Inc.

Bazerman, M., & Tenbrunsel, A. (2011). *Blind spots: Why we fail to do what's right and what to do about it.* Princeton, NJ: Princeton University Press.

BB&T (2012). Values. Retrieved January 5, 2012, from: http://www.bbt.com/about/philosophy/values.html

Benford, S., Bowers, J., Fahlen, L., Mariani, J., & Rodden, T. (1994). Supporting cooperative work in virtual environments. *The Computer Journal 37*(8), 653–668.

Bertland, A. (2009). Virtue ethics in business and the capabilities approach. *Journal of Business Ethics 84*(1), 25–32.

Birsch, D., & Fielder, J. (1994). *The Ford Pinto case: A study in applied ethics, business, and technology.* Albany, NY: State University of New York Press.

Bowie, N. (1998a). A Kantian theory of meaningful work. *Journal of Business Ethics 17*(9/10), 1083–1092.

Bowie, N. (1998b). A Kantian theory of capitalism. *Business Ethics Quarterly*, The Ruffin Series, Issue 1, 37–60.

Brenkert, G. (1981). Privacy, polygraphs, and work. *Business and Professional Ethics Journal 1*(10), 19–36.

Brenkert, G (2000). Social product liability: The case of firearms manufacturers. *Business Ethics Quarterly 10*(1), 21–32.

Burns, J. M. (1978). *Leadership*. New York, NY: Harper and Row Publishing.

Burton, B., & Dunn, C., (1996). Feminist ethics as a moral grounding for stakeholder theory. *Business Ethics Quarterly 6*(2), 133–147.

Capital One (2012). *Financial literacy programs*. Retrieved January 5, 2012, from: http://www.capitalone.com/financial-education/financial-literacy-programs/

Carroll, A. B. (1991). The pyramid of corporate social responsibility: Towards the moral management of organizational stakeholders. *Business Horizons*, July–August.

Carroll, A. B. (1999). Corporate social responsibility: Evolution of a definitional construct. *Business and Society 38*(3), 268–295.

Clarkson, M. (1998). *The corporation and its stakeholders*. Toronto: University of Toronto Press.

Cohan, J. (2001). Towards a new paradigm in the ethics of women's advertising. *Journal of Business Ethics 33*(4), 323–337.

Colle, S., & Werhane, P. (2000). Moral motivation across ethical theories. *Journal of Business Ethics 81*(4), 751–764.

Collins, J., & Porras, J. (1994). *Built to last: Successful habits of visionary companies*. New York, NY: Harper Collins Books.

Deming, E. (1986). *Out of the crisis*. Cambridge, MA: MIT Press.

DesJardins, J. (1987). Privacy in employment. In G. Ezorsky (Ed.), *Moral rights in the workplace* (pp. 127–139). Albany, NY: State University of New York Press.

DesJardins, J. (2005). Sustainable business: Environmental responsibilities and business opportunities. In J. DesJardins & J. McCall (Eds.), *Contemporary issues in business ethics* (V ed.) (pp. 409–416). Belmont, CA: Wadsworth/Thomson Publishing.

DesJardins, J., & McCall, J. (2005). *Contemporary issues in business ethics* (Vth ed.). Belmont, CA: Wadsworth/Thomson Publishing.

Dill, W. (1975). Public participation in corporate planning: Strategic management in a Kibitzer's world. *Long-Range Planning 8*(1), 57–63.

Donaldson, T. (2005). Rights in the global market. In J. DesJardins & J. McCall (Eds.), *Contemporary issues in business ethics* (pp. 478–491). Belmont, CA: Wadsworth/Thomson Publishing.

Donaldson, T., & Preston, L. (1995). The stakeholder theory of the corporation: Concepts, evidence, and implications. *The Academy of Management Review 20*(1), 65–91.

Dowie, M. (1997, September/October). Pinto madness. *Mother Jones.*

Ferrell, O., LeClair, D., & Ferrell, L. (1998). The federal sentencing guidelines for organizations: A framework for ethical compliance. *Journal of Business Ethics 17*, 353–363.

Ford Motor Company (2010/2011). *Sustainability report 2010/11.* Retrieved January 5th, 2012, from: http://corporate.ford.com/microsites/sustainability-report-2010-11/issues-supply

Freeman, R. E. (1984). *Strategic management: A stakeholder approach.* Boston, MA: Harper Collins Publishing.

Freeman, R. E. (1994). The politics of stakeholder theory: Some future directions. *Business Ethics Quarterly 4*(4), 409–421.

Freeman, R. E. (2008). Managing for stakeholders. In A. Zakhem, D. Palmer, & M. Stoll (Eds.), *Stakeholder theory: Essential readings in ethical leadership and management.* New York, NY: Prometheus Books.

Freeman, R. E., & Phillips, R. (2002). Stakeholder theory: A libertarian defense. *Business Ethics Quarterly 12*(3), 331–349.

Freeman, R. E., Harrison J., Wicks, A., Parmar, B., & de Colle, S. (2010). *Stakeholder theory: State of the art.* Cambridge, UK: Cambridge University Press.

Freeman, R. E., Wicks, A., & Parmar, B. (2004). Stakeholder theory and "the corporate objective function" revisited. *Organizational Science 15*(3), 364–369.

Friedman, M. (1970, September 13). The social responsibility of business is to create profits. *The New York Times Magazine.*

Fukuyama, F. (1996). *Trust: The social virtues and the creation of prosperity.* New York, NY: Free Press Paperbacks.

George, B. (2003). *Authentic leadership: Rediscovering the secrets to creating lasting value.* Hoboken, NJ: Jossey-Bass Press.

Gilbert, D., & Rasche, A. (2007). Discourse ethics and social accountability: The ethics of SA 8000. *Business Ethics Quarterly 17*, 187–216.

Global Reporting Initiative. *GRI Sustainability Reporting Guidelines G3.1 Reference Sheet.* http://www.globalreporting.org/NR/rdonlyres/D8B503A9-070C-43DB-AD0F-5C4ACB1EBF39/0/G31RefSheet.pdf

Goodin, R. (1985). *Protecting the vulnerable: A reanalysis of our social responsibilities.* Chicago, IL: University of Chicago Press.

Goodpaster, K. (1991). Business ethics and stakeholder analysis. *Business Ethics Quarterly 1*(1), 53–73.

Goodpaster, K., & Holloran, T. (1994). In defense of a paradox. *Business Ethics Quarterly 4*(4), 423–430.

Great Place to Work (2011). *World's best multi-national workplaces.* Retrieved January 5, 2012, from: http://www.greatplacetowork.com/best-companies/worlds-best-multinationals/list-of-the-25-best-from-2011

Habermas, J. (1984). *Theory of communicative action* (Vol. I.). Translated by T. McCarthy. Boston, MA: Beacon Press.

Habermas, J. (1987). *Theory of communicative action* (Vol. II.). Translated by T. McCarthy. Boston, MA: Beacon Press.

Habermas, J. (1990). *Moral consciousness and communicative action.* Cambridge, MA: MIT Press.

Habermas, J. (1993). *Justification and application: Remarks on discourse ethics.* Translated by C. Cronin. Cambridge, MA: The MIT Press.

Hess, D. (2007). A business ethics perspective on Sarbanes Oxley and the organizational sentencing guidelines. *Michigan Law Review 105*(8), 1781–1816.

International Organization for Standardization (2001). *Quality management system principles.* Retrieved from: http://www.iso.org/iso/qmp.htm

International Organization for Standardization (2008). *ISO 9001: 2008. Quality Management Systems—Requirements.* Published by the International Organization for Standardization.

Izraeli, D., & Schwartz, M. (1998). What can we learn from the U.S. Federal sentencing guidelines for organizational ethics? *Journal of Business Ethics 17*, 1045–1055.

Jackall, R. (1998). *Moral mazes: The world of corporate managers.* Oxford, UK: Oxford University Press.

Jackson, K. (1997). Globalizing ethics corporate ethics programs: Perils and prospects. *Journal of Business Ethics 16*, 1227–1235.

Laszlo, C. (2008). *Sustainable value: How the world's leading companies are doing well by doing good.* Stanford, CA: Stanford Business Books.

Kaler, J. (2002). Morality and strategy in stakeholder identification. *Journal of Business Ethics 39*(1–2), 91–100.

Kant, I. (1998). *Groundwork of the metaphysic of morals.* Translated by M. Gregor & C. M. Korsgaard. Cambridge, UK: Cambridge University Press.

Kaplan, R., & Norton, D. (1996). *The balanced scorecard: Translating strategy into action.* Cambridge, MA: Harvard University Press.

Kaptein, M. (2008a). Developing and testing a measure for the ethical culture of organizations: The corporate ethics virtue model. *Journal of Organizational Behavior 29*, 923–947.

Kaptein, M. (2008b). Development of a measure of unethical behavior in the workplace: A stakeholder perspective. *Journal of Management 34*, 978–1008.

Kaptein, M., & Avelino, S. (2005). Measuring corporate integrity: A survey-based approach. *Corporate Governance 5*, 45–54.

Kausek, J. (2006). *The management system auditor's handbook.* Milwaukee, WI: ASQ Quality Press.

Kimberly-Clark (2012). *Working here.* Retrieved January 5th, 2012, from: http://www.kimberly-clark.com/Careers/WorkingHere/WorkingHere.aspx?id=1669

Laufer, W. (2006). Illusions of compliance and governance. *Corporate Governance* 6, 239–249.

Lippke, R. (1989). Work, privacy, and autonomy. *Public Affairs Quarterly 3*(4), 41–55.

Loe, T., Ferrell, L., & Mansfield, P. (2000). A review of empirical studies assessing ethical decision making in business. *Journal of Business Ethics 25*(3), 185–204.

Marcoux, A. (2003). A fiduciary argument against stakeholder theory. *Business Ethics Quarterly 1*(1), 1–24.

Marens, R. & Wicks, A. (1999). Getting real: Stakeholder theory, managerial practice, and the general irrelevance of fiduciary duties owed to shareholders. *Business Ethics Quarterly 9*(2), 272–293.

Martin, R. (2010, January–February). The age of consumer capitalism. *Harvard Business Review*.

McCall, J. (2005). Deceptive advertising. In J. DesJardins & J. McCall (Eds.), *Contemporary issues in business ethics* (Vth ed.) (pp. 332–337). Belmont, CA: Wadsworth/Thomson Publishing.

McKendall, M., DeMarr, B., & Jones-Rickers, C. (2002). Ethical compliance programs and corporate illegality: Testing the assumptions of the corporate sentencing guidelines. *Journal of Business Ethics 37*, 367–383.

Michaelson, C. (2006). Compliance and the illusion of ethical progress. *Journal of Business Ethics 66*, 241–251.

Mill, J. S. (2001). *Utilitarianism*. Indianapolis, IN: Hackett Publishing Company.

Mitchell, R., Agle, B., & Wood, D. (1997). Toward a stakeholder theory of identification and salience: Defining the principle of who and what really counts. *Academy of Management Review 22*(4), 853–886.

National Association of Corporate Directors (2012). Retrieved January 5, 2012 from: http://www.nacdonline.org/

Nussbaum, M. (2000). *Women and human development: The capabilities approach.* Cambridge, UK: Cambridge University Press.

OECD (2011). *OECD guidelines for multinational enterprises, 2011 edition.* Retrieved January 5, 2012, from OECD iLibrary: http://dx.doi.org/10.1787/9789264115415-en

Orlitzky, M., Schmidt, F., & Rynes, S. (2003). Corporate social and financial performance: A meta-analysis. *Organization Studies 23*(3), 403–441.

Paine, L. (1994, March–April). Managing for organizational integrity. *Harvard Business Review*, 106–117.

Palazzo, G., & Scherer, A. (2006). Communicative legitimacy as deliberation: A communicative framework. *Journal of Business Ethics 66*(1), 71–88.

Palmer, D., & Zakhem, A. (2001). Bridging the gap between theory and practice: Using the 1991 federal sentencing guidelines as a paradigm for ethics training. *Journal of Business Ethics 29*(1–2), 77–84.

Pedersen, L. (2009). See no evil: Moral sensitivity in the formulation of business problems. *Business Ethics: A European Review 18*(4), 335–348.

Phillips, R. (1997). Stakeholder theory and a principle of fairness. *Business Ethics Quarterly 7*(1), 57–66.

Phillips, R. (2003). Stakeholder legitimacy. *Business Ethics Quarterly 13*(1), 25–41.

Phillips, R., Freeman, RE., & Wicks, A. (2003). What stakeholder theory is not. *Journal of Business Ethics 13*(4), 479–502.

Pless, N., & Maak, T. (2008). Responsible leadership in a globalized world: A cosmopolitan perspective. In A. Scherer & G. Palazzo (Eds.), *Handbook of research on global corporate citizenship* (pp. 430–453). Cheltenham: Edward Elgar Publishing.

Porter, M., Lorsch, J., & Nohria, N. (2004). Seven surprises for CEOs. *Harvard Business Review 82*(10), 62–75.

R-BEC (2001). Ethics compliance management system standard. Reitaku University, Japan.

Rachels, J. (1975). Why privacy is important. *Philosophy and Public Affairs 4*(4), 323–333.

Rachels, J., & Rachels, S. (2011). *The elements of moral philosophy*. New York, NY: McGraw-Hill.

Rafalko, R. (1994). Remaking the corporation: The 1991 U.S. Sentencing guidelines. *Journal of Business Ethics 13*, 625–636.

Reed, D. (1999). Stakeholder management theory: A critical theory perspective. *Business Ethics Quarterly 9*, 453–483.

Renouard, C. (2011). Corporate social responsibility, utilitarianism, and the capabilities approach. *Journal of Business Ethics 98*(1), 85–97.

Reynolds, S., & Bowie, N. (2004). A Kantian perspective on the characteristics of ethics programs. *Business Ethics Quarterly 14*, 275–292.

Reynolds, M., & Yuthas, K. (2008). Moral discourse and corporate social responsibility reporting. *Journal of Business Ethics 78*(1–2), 47–65.

Sandberg, J. (2008a). The tide is turning on the separation thesis? *Business Ethics Quarterly 18*(4), 561–565.

Sandberg, J. (2008b). Understanding the separation thesis. *Business Ethics Quarterly 18*(2), 213–232.

Sen, A. (1993). Capability and well-being. In Nussbaum and Sen (Eds.), *The Quality of Life* (pp. 30–53). Oxford: Clarendon Press.

Sen, A. (2005). Human rights and capabilities. *Journal of Human Development 6*(2), 151–166.

Sen, A. (2009). *The idea of justice*. London: Allen Lane Publishing.

Solomon, R. (1997). *It's good business: Ethics and free enterprise for the new millennium*. Lanham, MD: Rowman and Littlefield Publishers.

Stansbury, J. (2009). Reasoned moral agreement: Applying discourse ethics within organizations. *Business Ethics Quarterly 19*(1), 33–56.

Starik, M. (1995). Should trees have managerial standing? Toward stakeholder status for non-human nature. *Journal of Business Ethics 14*, 207–218.

Stout, L. (2002). Bad and not-so-bad arguments for shareholder primacy. *Southern California Law Review 75*, 1189–1209.

Trevino, L., & Nelson, K. (1999). *Managing business ethics: Straight talk about how to do it right.* New York, NY: John Wiley and Sons Publishing.

United Nations General Assembly. (1948). Universal declaration of human rights. http://www.un.org/en/documents/udhr/

United States Federal Government. (2002). *Sarbanes Oxley Act.* http://www.soxlaw.com/index.htm

United States Sentencing Commission (2010). *2010 Federal sentencing guideline manual.* Retrieved from: http://www.ussc.gov/Guidelines/2010_guidelines/Manual_HTML/Chapter_8.htm

Valentine, S., Godkin, L., & Fleischman, G., (2011). Corporate ethical values, group creativity, job satisfaction, and turnover intention: The impact of context on work response. *Journal of Business Ethics 98*(3), 353–372.

Verschoor, C. (1998). A study of the link between a corporation's financial performance and its commitment to ethics. *Journal of Business Ethics 17*, 1509–1516.

Vos, J. (2003). Corporate social responsibility and the identification of stakeholders. *Corporate Social Responsibility and Environmental Management 10*(3), 141–152.

Wempe, B. (2008). Understanding the separation thesis: Precision after the decimal point? *Business Ethics Quarterly 18*(4), 549–553.

Werhane, P. (1999). *Moral imagination and management decision making.* Oxford, UK: Oxford University Press.

Werhane, P. (2002). Moral imagination and systems thinking. *Journal of Business Ethics 38*, 33–42.

Werhane, P. (2005). The right to due process. In J. DesJardins & J. McCall (Eds.), *Contemporary issues in business ethics* (V ed.) (pp. 136–141). Belmont, CA: Wadsworth/Thomson Publishing.

Wicks, A., Gilbert, D., & Freeman, R. E. (1994). A feminist reinterpretation of the stakeholder concept. *Business Ethics Quarterly 4*(4), 475–497.

Zakhem, A. (2008). Stakeholder management theory: A discourse ethical approach. *Journal of Business Ethics 79*(4), 395–405.

Index

Announcing the Business Expert Press Digital Library

Concise E-books Business Students Need for Classroom and Research

This book can also be purchased in an e-book collection by your library as

- a one-time purchase,
- that is owned forever,
- allows for simultaneous readers,
- has no restrictions on printing, and
- can be downloaded as PDFs from within the library community.

Our digital library collections are a great solution to beat the rising cost of textbooks. e-books can be loaded into their course management systems or onto student's e-book readers.

The **Business Expert Press** digital libraries are very affordable, with no obligation to buy in future years. For more information, please visit **www.businessexpertpress.com/librarians**. To set up a trial in the United States, please contact **Adam Chesler** at *adam.chesler@businessexpertpress.com* for all other regions, contact **Nicole Lee** at *nicole.lee@igroupnet.com*.

OTHER TITLES IN OUR STRATEGIC MANAGEMENT COLLECTION

Collection Editor: William Q. Judge

- *Building Strategy and Performance Through Time: The Critical Path* by Kim Warren
- *Sustainable Business: An Executive's Primer* by Nancy Landrum and Sally Edwards
- *Mergers and Acquisitions: Turmoil in Top Management Teams* by Jeffrey Krug
- *Positive Management: Increasing Employee Productivity* by Jack Walters
- *Business Goes Virtual: Realizing the Value of Collaboration, Social and Virtual Strategies* by John Girard and JoAnn Girard
- *Fundamentals of Global Strategy: A Business Model Approach* by Cornelis de Kluyver
- *Grow by Focusing on What Matters: Competitive Strategy in 3-Circles* by Joe Urbany and Jim Davis
- *Operational Leadership* by Andrew Spanyi
- *Succeeding at the Top: A Self-Paced Workbook for Newly Appointed CEOs and Executives* by Bernard Liebowitz
- *Achieving Excellence in Management: Identifying and Learning from Bad Practices* by Andrew Kilner
- *Building Organizational Capacity for Change: The Leader's New Mandate* by William Q. Judge
- *Business Intelligence: Making Decisions Through Data Analytics* by Jerzy Surma